KU-607-571

AN INTRODUCTION TO THE PHILOSOPHY OF EDUCATION

by

D. J. O'CONNOR

LONDON

ROUTLEDGE & KEGAN PAUL

First published in 1957
by Routledge & Kegan Paul Ltd
Broadway House, 68-74 Carter Lane
London EC4V 5EL
© *D. F. O'Connor*, 1957
Printed in Great Britain by
Compton Printing Ltd
London & Aylesbury
Second impression 1958
Third impression 1961
Fourth impression 1963
Fifth impression 1965
Sixth impression 1967
Seventh impression 1968
Eighth impression 1969
Ninth impression 1971
ISBN 0 7100 1898 3(c)
ISBN 0 7100 4664 2(p)

PREFACE

THIS book has two purposes. In the first place, it is intended to be a primer of the philosophy of education. I take this to mean that it should examine, in an elementary way, the most obvious points of contact between philosophy and educational theory. Secondly, I have tried to develop the philosophical questions so as to provide a simple introduction to philosophical thinking for those students of education in universities and training colleges who would otherwise have no formal contact with philosophy.

The viewpoint represented here is that of contemporary 'philosophical analysis'. This label does not, as is often supposed, apply to a single 'school' of philosophy but is used to refer to the work of a large number of philosophers of very widely differing views. However, they do share certain attitudes and ways of thinking which have not yet been sufficiently represented in writings on education. Indeed, the only previous attempt of this kind, so far as I am aware, is Professor C. D. Hardie's excellent little book *Truth and Fallacy in Educational Theory* published in 1942 and now out of print.

Because it has not been usual for analytical philosophers to write about such matters, important contemporary ideas are still unfamiliar to educational theorists and students of education. This is a pity because philosophy in its present form has important bearings on all our theoretical enterprises. Its main ideas should therefore be made known as widely as possible. The exposition here is very elementary and therefore rather unsubtle; but I have tried to supplement this short book with bibliographical notes that will enable the student who wishes to pursue any topic to find the easiest way to do so.

Preface

I am glad to record my thanks to friends at the University College of North Staffordshire who gave me some very helpful criticisms: Professor A. G. N. Flew, Mr. Alan Montefiore and Professor W. A. Campbell Stewart whose seminars first interested me in these questions. I am especially grateful to Miss Hazel Bennett of the same college who was kind enough to tell me what a first-year student thought of an early draft of this book.

D. J. O'C.

Department of Philosophy,
University of Liverpool,
June 1956.

CONTENTS

I

PHILOSOPHY AND EDUCATION

I

THE phrase 'philosophy of education' occurs commonly in writings about the theory and practice of education. It is however not always obvious what it means. Often, indeed, if we look critically at the uses of phrases like 'the philosophy of education', 'the philosophical basis of education', 'philosophical presuppositions of educational theory' and so on, it becomes clear that they are no more than vague though high-sounding titles for miscellaneous talk about the aims and methods of teaching. Such usages could well be dropped in the interests of clarity. But I certainly do not want to suggest that language of this sort has no proper and useful function. Phrases like 'philosophy of science', 'philosophy of history' or 'philosophy of art' are also used from time to time in a pretentious or muddle-headed way. Yet they can be used to refer to genuine and important fields of enquiry.

Even a non-technical use of the word 'philosophy' in such contexts may be helpful if it is made clear. Sir Godfrey Thomson, in his well-known book *A Modern Philosophy of Education*, explains that he uses the word 'philosophy' in the title merely 'to indicate that I wish to look at education as a whole, and try to make as consistent and sensible an idea of that whole as I can'.[1] Again, the word may occur in such phrases as 'a Christian philosophy of education'. Here it often

[1] Op. cit., p. 11.

I

means no more than 'guiding values or ideals' as when we talk colloquially of 'a philosophy of life'. Neither of these senses of the word have much connexion with the technical meaning with which we shall be concerned in discussing the philosophy of education. Yet there are ways in which philosophy as a specialized discipline is very relevant to education. And I want to try to work out in this short essay the main ways in which philosophy, in this sense of the word, and educational theory and practice are related. For I believe that philosophical methods and findings can be of service to educational theorists and students of education, just as they can be of service to scientists, literary critics, historians or theologians. But they cannot be of service unless the nature of philosophy *and its limitations* are first understood.

In this first chapter, I shall try to give an outline account of the respective spheres of philosophy and education. This will enable us to see the possible points of contact between the two subjects. My account of the aims and methods of philosophy will be very sketchy and directed rather to get rid of misconceptions than to give any positive information. I shall have to amplify and justify what I say, at some length, in later chapters.[1] In what I say about education, I shall be occupied only in stating some familiar platitudes that may serve to indicate the points with which this chapter is concerned and to clear the ground for future discussion.

II

When a student begins the study of philosophy, he is often surprised to find that much of his time is taken up with getting acquainted with the opinions of the philosophers of the past, in some cases, men who lived well over two thousand years ago. This seems surprising because in subjects like mathematics and chemistry the history of a particular theorem or hypothesis is usually only of incidental interest. Our interest in the theorem of Pythagoras does not arise from the fact that Pythagoras or Euclid first stated and proved it at a certain

[1] See, in particular, Chapters 2 and 3.

stage in the history of mathematics. We are interested in it because it follows validly from the foundations of Euclidean geometry and has many useful applications in our everyday world. The ground of our interest in Boyle's law is not that Boyle first formulated it in the seventeenth century but that it describes more or less accurately the way in which gases behave under pressure. If a particular scientific hypothesis such as the caloric theory of heat or the phlogiston theory of combustion is disproved, it is discarded from the body of science and survives, if at all, only as an historical curiosity.

But the student of philosophy learns philosophy to a large extent from the history of his subject. Experience has shown that it is not easy to teach it in any other way, at least to beginners. And here he is further surprised to find that he is not taught the opinions of Plato, Aristotle, Descartes and the rest because they are universally accepted as true. On the contrary, he finds that very few, if any, philosophical doctrines are generally held by philosophers and that he learns what Plato said about knowledge or what Descartes said about the relation between mind and body only, so it seems, to refute them. A large part of undergraduate courses in philosophy consists in destructive criticism of the opinions of the great philosophers from Socrates to Russell. It is not only the student of philosophy who is impressed by the seemingly negative and unprogressive character of philosophical enquiry. Philosophers themselves have tried to find remedies for it from time to time or have tried at least to explain it. And there have been plenty of cynical or sceptical critics who have pointed to the activities of philosophers as evidence that the very hope that philosophy might give knowledge or enlightenment of any kind is a chimerical one. But this sceptical attitude results from misunderstanding the significance of the critical activities of philosophers. Indeed, its significance has been appreciated by philosophers themselves only in quite recent years. The work of Professor G. E. Moore and of Lord Russell in the early years of this century was the first stage of a revolution in philosophy that is still in progress. It is rash to try to

3

summarize the effects of a contemporary movement of this kind but the work of leading philosophers in recent years has made it clear that philosophy is not a body of knowledge of a positive kind like history or botany or law.

In the past, both philosophers and their critics made the mistake of assuming that philosophy was a kind of superior science that could be expected to answer difficult and important questions about human life and man's place and prospects in the universe. In particular, philosophers tried to answer questions of the following kinds: Is there a God and, if so, what, if anything, can we learn by reason about His nature? Do human beings survive their death? Are we free to choose our own courses of action or are human actions events in a causal series over which we can have no control? By what standards are we to judge human actions as right or wrong? How are these standards themselves to be justified?

I said above that it was a mistake to assume that philosophy was a sort of superior and profounder science whose findings would give the answers to questions like these. In saying this, I am putting forward a philosophical theory which, like all such theories, finds no general acceptance. Nevertheless, it can be made very plausible and part of my task in the following chapters will be to explain and defend this view of philosophy and show how it can throw some light on the problems of education. It is a view which is very widely accepted in one form or another at the present day. And even those philosophers who do not accept it have modified their opinions and their methods under its influence. I shall give an elementary account of this view of philosophy in Chapter 2. Elsewhere, I shall try to show some of its uses in practice. For the present it will be sufficient to state that in this view, philosophy is not in the ordinary sense of the phrase a body of knowledge but rather an activity of criticism or clarification. As such, it can be exercised on any subject matter at all, including our present concern, the problems of educational theory.

4

III

It is a good deal easier to understand the nature, aims and methods of education. In one sense of 'education', we all know very well what it means. The word refers to the sort of training that goes on in schools and universities and so on. But it is not this sense of the word with which we are now concerned. When a student at a university or a training college is said to be studying education, he is not interested only in the very diverse kinds of activities that go on in schools and colleges. The word 'education' has a wider meaning for him, a meaning that can be summarily expressed as follows:

'Education' refers to:

(a) a set of techniques for imparting knowledge, skills and attitudes;

(b) a set of theories which purport to explain or justify the use of these techniques;

(c) a set of values or ideals embodied and expressed in the purposes for which knowledge, skills and attitudes are imparted and so directing the amounts and types of training that is given.

It is the third element (c) that is most clearly relevant to philosophy. This is because (a) and (b), the techniques of teaching and the theories that explain and justify them, are matters that can be determined only by the methods of the positive sciences and in particular, the science of psychology. The question of what techniques are most effective for teaching arithmetic or geography or anything else is *a question of fact* to be determined by observation, refined by experiment and aided by statistical devices for weighing the evidence obtained. There is no other way of settling such questions. Again, the theories of the educational psychologists about such matters as learning, motivation, the nature and distribution of intelligence, child development and so on are (or ought to be) the theoretical basis on which particular educational techniques or administrative methods are recommended or explained. These theories are part of a science and must be established, if they are to be of any value at all, by the methods appropriate to a science. Philosophy has nothing whatever to do with proving such factual questions. There is however one way in which philosophy may be of service even here. It is not always obvious to students of a science exactly what is the relation of the scientific theories which they study to the facts that support the theories and which the theories are said to explain. Even in the case of the physical sciences, this relation between fact and theory is not always clear to the student, though in these sciences it is usually easiest to understand. And in the case of the biological and social sciences the relations between the facts of experience and the explanatory superstructure of theory is often much more complex and difficult. Now these questions about the nature of theories and their explanatory function are philosophical questions. I shall therefore have something to say in Chapter 5 about the function of educational theories.

Nevertheless, it is the questions of value raised by (*c*) that are felt most acutely as problems by the student of education and the educational theorist. And on these questions too, philosophy can help, at least to the extent of showing what the problems are and explaining their special character. We can best introduce this matter by considering the question of the aims of education implicit in (*c*) above. It is obviously the most important question that can be asked on this topic. For upon the *detailed* answer that is given will depend the whole of the organization and teaching practice of a society. Different ends usually require different means, in education as elsewhere. What then can usefully be said about the aims and objects of education?

There is a sense in which the aim of education must be the same in all societies. Two hundred years from now there will be no one alive in the world who is alive here today. Yet the sum total of human skill and knowledge will probably not be less than it is today. It will almost certainly be greater. And that this is so is due in large part to the educational process by

6

which we pass on to one generation what has been learned and achieved by previous generations. The continuity and growth of society is obviously dependent in this way upon education, both formal and informal. If each generation had to learn for itself what had been learned by its predecessor, no sort of intellectual or social development would be possible and the present state of society would be little different from the society of the old stone age. But this basic aim of education is so general and so fundamental that it is hardly given conscious recognition as an educational *purpose*. It is rather to be classed as the most important social *function* of education and is a matter of interest to the sociologist rather than to the educational theorist. Education does this job in any society and the specific way in which it does it will vary from one society to another. When we speak in the ordinary way about the aims of education, we are interested rather in the specific goals set by the nature of the society and the purposes of its members.

The educational system of any society is a more or less elaborate social mechanism designed to bring about in the persons submitted to it certain skills and attitudes that are judged to be useful and desirable in the society. Ultimately, all the questions that can be asked about a given educational system can be reduced to two: (i) What is held to be valuable as an end? (ii) What means will effectively realize these ends? Now if in order to answer this question about the aims of education, it were necessary to survey all the philosophical problems connected with valuation and all the sociological questions about the most effective policies for achieving different ends, it would not be possible to write concisely about the relations between philosophy and education at all. But fortunately, as the question arises in any society, we can take for granted a lot of common ground even between those people who differ most sharply between themselves on education and its aims. For the ordinary day-to-day working of the society itself makes it necessary for its members to have a certain minimum of skills and attitudes in common. And the imparting of this common minimum is one of the ends of education.

7

The question 'What is this minimum?' will be answered differently in different societies. In twentieth-century England, reading, writing and a respect for the law would be a part of the common minimum. In a South Pacific island, swimming, fish-spearing and a respect for one's elders might be more in place.

I propose then to give a tentative list of the aims of education in order to bring out one of the important points of contact between philosophy and education, the issue of the nature and validity of value judgments. I shall purposely make my list neither so specific as to be uselessly controversial nor so vague as to give us no guide to action. To talk of education in Dewey's words as 'a constant reorganizing or reconstructing of experience', or in Thomson's as 'the influence of the environment upon the individual to produce a permanent change in his habits of behaviour, of thought and of attitude', is to be too general. We need not suppose that we are trying to give a 'real' or 'true' definition of the concept we are concerned with. All we need to do here is to describe in fairly precise and recognizable terms the aims of the social process called 'education' with which we are all, to some degree, familiar from our own experience. When these aims are expressed in general terms, they can form a convenient basis on which educational theorists of the most diverse views can all agree. But as soon as we begin to elaborate some of these aims and specify them more precisely, differences of opinion on their interpretation are bound to arise. With this proviso about the limitations of such a catalogue, I shall list the aims of education as follows:

1 to provide men and women with a minimum of the skills necessary for them (*a*) to take their place in society and (*b*) to seek further knowledge;
2 to provide them with a vocational training that will enable them to be self-supporting;
3 to awaken an interest in and a taste for knowledge;
4 to make them critical;

5 to put them in touch with and train them to appreciate the
cultural and moral achievements of mankind.

Such a list as this may seem merely one more of the edifying
platitudes that are so apt to occur in writings on education.
My purpose in producing (or reproducing) here a programme
of this sort is partly to try to clarify the main points of contact between philosophy and education so that I can show what
help the student of education may expect from the activities
of the philosopher. For the purposes of my argument, it is
immaterial whether it is claimed that these are the 'real' aims
or that they *ought to be* the aims of any system of education. I
am saying merely that these aims do as a matter of fact command a wide measure of assent among persons interested in
such matters. It will be obvious too that some of these aims
can be realized at fairly primitive levels of education while
others can be achieved only imperfectly even at very advanced
levels. Nevertheless, such are among some of the most important aims of an educational system in any civilized country.

But if we look more closely at the list, it is easy to see that a
more precise specification of its contents soon gives occasion
for disagreement. The following remarks to explain and
amplify the items of the list may therefore be regarded merely
as my own recommendations for interpreting a set of rather
abstractly stated ends in a more detailed and therefore more
practical way. Any such interpretation will make clear the
valuations of the interpreter. But as practically any set of value
judgments raises much the same philosophical problems, it
matters very little which set we take as illustrative. The important thing to notice is that any such list of educational aims
must embody, however carefully they may be disguised, the
valuations of its proposer. Like superstitions, valuations are
dangerous unless they are recognized for what they are.

1   *The minimum skills:* This is the least controversial of the
listed aims. In most civilized societies, constituted as they are
at present, men and women must know how to read and write
and calculate sufficiently to get through their ordinary daily

business. And those of them who have the interest and ability to be technicians or scientists or scholars or artists, will need to develop these elementary skills to a much higher level. They may need, for example, to read and write more than one language and to have a better command of their own or to have at their disposal techniques of calculation far beyond those of simple arithmetic.

2 *Vocational training:* At its simplest level, this aim will overlap the first. To be able to live as useful members of a society, we must in general be capable of supporting ourselves. Many jobs will always be unskilled and many others can be learned only by doing them. But where the organization of a society is technically complex, a large number of the skilled occupations will always presuppose in the novices who enter on them a considerable body of theoretical knowledge and practical skills. Even to start training to be a doctor or an engineer, a boy must know a good deal of elementary science and mathematics that cannot usually be acquired in less than four or five years of school.

The relation between technological training and higher education is often considered a matter for controversy. But the controversy is largely a verbal one between those to whom 'technologist' is a term of opprobrium and those to whom it is a name of honour. Few people, after all, would dispute that there are some technical skills like plumbing or servicing motor-cars that do not presuppose a training at a university level while others like operating for appendicitis or building a suspension bridge do need such a training. This is the only question of fact relevant to the controversy.

3 *Awakening the desire for knowledge:* If we accept this as an end for education, it will probably be because we agree that the acquisition of knowledge and its advancement are in some way valuable in themselves and not merely because they offer the means to increased profits, comfort or prestige. Now this is a judgment of value that may very well be challenged. And it is not easy to see how it is to be defended or justified or

even what sort of a defence or justification, if any, it requires. These are, in the first place, problems for the philosopher. I do not mean to say that philosophers are called upon to 'prove' or 'validate' or 'justify' this particular judgment or, indeed, any other. But it is part of their job to scrutinize very carefully the puzzling features that such statements present and to propose analyses of them that will make it easier to see what is being claimed by those who uphold a particular value judgment and what is being denied by those who reject it. It is only when these things have been made clear that the dispute can be settled, if it ever can.

4 *Developing a critical outlook:* To make men critical is not as widely held to be a good thing as to make them love knowledge. And it is obvious why this is so. The patrons and organizers of education are normally political or religious bodies, states and churches, who cannot in their own interest encourage a catholic and indiscriminate taste for the sceptical examination of claims and authorities. It is a matter of history that the sceptic is rarely in favour with those in power and is usually looked on as a disrupting and revolutionary influence. But it is equally a matter of history that advances in knowledge, morality or social organization would happen slowly, if they happened at all, without the stimulus of astringent and questioning minds.

Since to make men critical is only to teach them to proportion the degree of their various beliefs to the weight of the evidence in their favour it is difficult to understand how it can properly be deprecated as an educational aim. It is, to be sure, often set down by theorists (as I am setting it down here) as an end of education. But its neglect in practice leads us to suppose that, like most moral rules, it is more inspiring and comforting as an unrealized ideal than as a way of life. This then is another value judgment; one of the primary ends of education is to make men critical. It therefore marks another point at which the philosopher may help to clarify the difficulties that confront the educator.

11

It is perhaps worth pointing out once again a practical justification for the critical habit of mind. A passion for certainty seems to be innate in human beings. This strong natural tendency is, in part, the source of all the human achievements in enquiry and exploration from those of the scientists and scholars to those of the great explorers. But equally, it is, in part, the source of all human dogmatisms and fanaticisms. We are so anxious to know the truth that we are ready to welcome its semblance without the evidence that is its only possible credential. A moderately sceptical outlook can prevent us from deceiving ourselves in this way. And it can do this without hindering the genuine advance of knowledge which must, in any case, wait for its evidence before it is admitted into the body of rational belief. The critical habit of mind is merely the virtue of self-restraint exercised upon the passion for certainty. And like most virtues it can point to the happy results of its practice. Self-indulgence in our desire for certainty is no less dangerous and degrading, though far more respectable than its other forms.

This is worth emphasizing at the present time when the esteem in which reason is held among civilized men is undergoing one of its periodic eclipses. G. K. Chesterton once made the characteristic remark that the purpose of an open mind like that of an open mouth was to close it firmly on something. This shows a common misunderstanding of the quality of critical openmindedness. An openminded man is not a man who never makes up his mind but one who never does so finally and irrevocably. His beliefs and decisions are always subject to revision in the light of further evidence. The critical habit of mind lies in the willingness to recognize that no evidence can be so conclusive as to make further evidence irrelevant.

5   *The appreciation of human achievements:* That educated men and women should have some knowledge and appreciation of what is best in literature, art, music, science and the rest of the apparatus of higher civilization is an educational platitude so banal that it seems hardly worth recording. And it is no less

a platitude that education should include *some* sort of moral training. But the excuse for reaffirming these obvious truths is that they are important. Like the statements of the other aims of education, they turn from truisms to controversial opinions as soon as we try to specify their content at all exactly. We need not try to do that here. I mention them as important educational ends in which the interests of the teacher, the educational theorist and the philosopher are all involved. In recognizing these ends at all, we cannot escape making or at least presupposing moral and aesthetic valuations. And in making such valuations we are making claims whose exact content is obscure and difficult to clarify. Their clarification is part of the philosopher's work.

IV

The nature of value judgments and the logic of their justification is thus the most important and most obvious point of contact between philosophy and education and I shall discuss this in some detail in Chapter 3. There are however other ways in which philosophy may be of help to the educational theorist. Theories about education are often very complex mixtures of different sorts of statement. Because of this, the language in which they are expressed is easily misunderstood both by students of the theories and even by their authors. The difficulty in understanding these theories is not always due to the defects in their presentation, though it is true that the moral earnestness so patent in much educational writing is often the worst enemy of clarity. These theories are more often hard to understand because their authors fail to make clear what kind of a theory it is and what it is expected to do. Educational theories are not all of the same kind and cannot all be judged in the same way. It is one of the philosopher's jobs to try to elucidate such theories and assess their logical worth and their explanatory function. Questions about the criticism and elucidation of theories in education will be discussed in Chapters 4 and 5.

The elementary discussion of the nature of philosophy in the second chapter has two purposes. It is intended to give the reader who knows nothing about philosophy a brief and necessarily inadequate account of the way in which the development of knowledge has led to a changed outlook in philosophy. It is also designed to remove some common misunderstandings about the relation of philosophy to other fields of study. These misunderstandings sometimes lead to exaggerated claims being made for 'the philosophy of science', 'the philosophy of history' or 'the philosophy of education' and to bewilderment or disillusion among the victims of such claims. A proper comprehension of what philosophy can and cannot do for another discipline can have a useful deflationary effect in this respect and, more important, will direct attention to the very real services that philosophical criticism *can* perform. And finally, the study of philosophy by increasing our sensitivity to logical distinctions and the multifarious workings of language can enable us to distinguish more easily between different kinds of statement and the different kinds of evidence appropriate to each. And this kind of sensitivity is a very useful qualification for any kind of theoretical activity.

In the chapters which follow I shall try to confine myself to those main questions of philosophy which have a direct bearing on educational theories. Most writers on the philosophy of education interpret their task more widely than this. For example, Dewey's well-known introduction to the subject, *Democracy and Education* discusses questions of psychology, of sociology and of educational method. Moreover the early chapters contain a good deal of acute discussion on the nature and aims of education which does not fall obviously into any conventional academic province. Discussions of all these questions are, of course, interesting and valuable to students of education but it is a pity to suggest that they are philosophical. One of the most important and difficult tasks for the student who is beginning philosophy is to understand the difference between philosophical questions on the one hand and questions of logic, history, science or commonsense fact on the other. I shall try at least to make this distinction clear by understanding the phrase 'philosophy of education' to mean 'those problems of philosophy that are of direct relevance to educational theory'. It will not be possible to deal with all these questions. But an elementary discussion of some of the important ones will make clear what a philosophical question is like. And this will at least ensure that the reader will be able to recognize philosophy when he meets it and so be safeguarded against one of the commonest and most dangerous of intellectual errors—that of talking philosophy unawares.

2

THE NATURE OF PHILOSOPHY

I

THE work of the philosopher has traditionally been supposed
to consist of three connected tasks. In the first place, he has
been expected to provide a compendious overall view of the
universe and of man's place in it. Secondly, he has been expected to do this by rational procedures and not, for example,
by intuition or poetic imagination. Lastly, men have looked to
the philosopher to give them or at least justify for them, a
religious point of view that would also be defensible by reason.
Philosophers have thus been expected to combine the aims and
achievements of scientists, moralists and theologians. But these
expectations have proved far beyond what they have been able
to accomplish. On rare occasions, a philosopher of genius like
Aquinas[1] or Spinoza[2] has given us a map of the universe that
many people have found both intellectually and spiritually
satisfying. But in such cases it has proved only too easy for the
philosopher's critics to attack the logic of his system or the
truth of his premisses. They have shown in this way that, however fascinating and persuasive his picture of the world may be,
there is no good reason to believe that it is a true one.

At the present day, philosophers would state their aims very

[1] St. Thomas Aquinas (1225–74), a medieval theologian and
philosopher.
[2] Baruch Spinoza (1632–77), a Jewish philosopher who lived
in Holland.

16

much more modestly though, naturally enough, a philosopher's view of the scope of his discipline will depend on his own philosophical opinions. A few of them might still want to maintain the traditional view. But most would agree that the traditional philosophers promised more than they were able to deliver and that their claims to interpret the universe on a grand scale must be rejected for just the same reason that the claims of alchemists, astrologers or magicians are now rejected. The reason is the simple and fundamental one that the results of any sort of enquiry are acceptable in so far as they are publicly testable, reliable and coherent with the rest of public knowledge. Traditional metaphysics,[1] like astrology and alchemy, cannot meet these requirements. It may perhaps be objected that the requirements themselves are arbitrary if they are applied to philosophy since these are standards by which

[1] The word 'metaphysics' occurs here for the first time. As it will be used several times in the course of this book, it may be useful to explain the sense in which it will be understood. A statement is metaphysical if it assumes the existence of entities or facts which lie outside the range of human observation and experience. An argument is metaphysical if it purports to prove the existence of such entities or facts. Note that statements are not metaphysical because they cannot *in fact* be checked by observation, but because they cannot *in principle* be checked in this way. Compare the following statements: (1) On January 1st, 1567, there were 6537 crocodiles in the River Zambesi. (2) Some good actions are the result of divine grace. (3) Julius Caesar had blood belonging to group AB. (4) Julius Caesar had an immortal soul. (2) and (4) are metaphysical; (1) and (3) are not, because, although we do not know whether they are true and can never find out, the sort of evidence which would confirm them is within the range of human observation.

Examples of metaphysical statements of a more serious kind will be found on pages 41–42. This book will not intentionally contain metaphysical statements except as illustrative examples. But the reader should realize that not all metaphysical statements are as easy to recognize as (2) and (4) above and that the questions 'What is a metaphysical statement?' and 'How far are such statements meaningful?' are still live and debatable issues in philosophy. The explanation of the term 'metaphysical' given above is a very rough clarification which will serve our present purposes.

we test scientific knowledge. We may return to this objection at the end of the chapter after we have looked at the way in which philosophy has developed.

The history of western philosophy started in fifth-century Greece. If we examine the doctrines of the Greek philosophers, we see that they cover an enormously wide field. We find discussions of characteristically philosophical problems like the existence of God, the nature of human knowledge and the good life for man. We also find interest in questions of mathematics and astronomy, physics and chemistry of a primitive kind, biology and the social sciences. Moreover we do not find that any clear distinction was made between those questions that we nowadays recognize as philosophical and those that we class as scientific. Not only was knowledge not departmentalized as it is today but it was not even divided into the main *logically distinct types of enquiry* that we now recognize. We distinguish nowadays between physics, chemistry and zoology, for example, but this kind of distinction is largely a matter of administrative convenience, so to speak. The field of scientific knowledge has become far too detailed and complex for one man to deal effectively with more than a very small area. The division and subdivision of natural science into specialities is thus a practical device to meet the limitations of man's mind and the shortness of his life. There is however a more basic distinction between branches of knowledge. This depends not on the kind of material that we study but on the *sort of evidence* by which we advance our knowledge. Botanists study plants, geologists the history and structure of the earth's crust, astronomers the planets and stars. But all of them get their material by observing nature through the senses. Indeed this is one of the characteristic features of the sciences. Pure mathematics and formal logic on the other hand do not derive their material from observation of the world nor are the findings of these sciences proved or supported by this kind of evidence. Anyone who has taken a school course of elementary geometry is aware that we do not *prove* that the three angles of a plane triangle total two right angles by drawing a selection of triangles and measuring their angles. We prove such propositions by deductions from axioms or postulates conventionally accepted as a starting point. And when we turn to the problems of philosophy, it is easy to see that they cannot be decided either by the observational methods of the natural sciences or the deductive methods of mathematics and formal logic. For if they were decidable in this way, some of them at least would long since have been decided. (It is not merely a truism to say that *what is provable can be proved*. Indeed, we can read in this statement one reason for the failure of traditional metaphysics and natural religion.)

This very important logical point that different kinds of statement demand different kinds of evidence is not one that the Greek or medieval philosophers would have denied if it had been put to them. They were, in a sense, aware of the point but the presuppositions of their thinking and the state of knowledge in their time did not require them to bring it into focus and concede it any importance. But this situation was radically altered by the rise of natural science and the renaissance of mathematics during the seventeenth and eighteenth centuries.

All the sciences started as branches of philosophy in the sense that the Greek word 'philosophia' was originally used in a very general sense to cover all investigations into the nature of man and of the universe. But in the sixteenth and seventeenth centuries a discovery was made about scientific method which seems to us nowadays trivial and obvious, perhaps because it is the unquestioned foundation of a civilization based on the achievements of natural science. This was the discovery that if you want to know what the world is like, you have to look and see. As a practical maxim, this was not always a commonplace. There have been long periods in the history of the world and no doubt there will be again, when people were discouraged from looking either by the intellectual fashions of their time or because the prevailing religious or political outlook might conflict with what observation would tell them.

And of course mere observation of the world of nature was not enough to lay the foundations of science. The results of observation had to be refined by experiment and by measurement and the direction of observation controlled by hypothesis. But once men had learned the lesson of what has been called 'respect for fact', natural science started on that brilliant epoch of development which has marked off the last three hundred years from all other periods of history. This lesson was first thoroughly, though slowly, learned by the scientists of western Europe during the seventeenth and eighteenth centuries.

Thus science became emancipated from philosophy by the discovery of its proper method; and the only relic of the long association between the two is the title of 'Professor of Natural Philosophy' which adorns the holders of chairs of physics in some of the older British universities. The method of observation and experiment had of course been practised in Greek and medieval times but in a half-hearted and sporadic way; and it had not usually been practised in conjunction with the language of mathematics, the language in which, in Galileo's famous epigram, the book of nature is written. But with the systematic adoption of the experimental method and the translation of natural laws into mathematical modes of expression, men were at last developing a large body of reliable and testable knowledge. They were moreover acquiring it with the aid of a method whose power they recognized and which they consciously applied to the solution of the problems of nature. Philosophers could now compare the uncertain powers of their own speculative methods with the method of hypothesis and experiment. Though it is a method that needs slow, laborious and piecemeal application, it gives answers that can be progressively corrected, tested and communicated and leads in the end to generally accepted results. Like many other important revolutions, this one did not take place overnight. Indeed its full impact has not been felt by all educated men even at the present day. But most philosophers since the seventeenth century, many of whom were also men of science, saw clearly enough what the new way of explaining the world meant for them. It was a challenge to find a method of tackling the problems of philosophy which would be appropriate to those problems and so would enable men to agree when a solution of them had been reached.

There is one important way in which the success of the natural scientists helped the philosophers to focus their difficulties more clearly. It became obvious with the rise of the scientific method that the attention of philosophers in ancient and medieval times sometimes had been taken up with questions that had not properly been matters for them at all, since they were questions decidable only by the methods of the scientists. Aristotle, for example, discussed not only philosophical questions such as origins of human knowledge, the nature of morality and the relations between mind and body but also scientific questions about the mechanism of sensation, the constitution of the physical universe, the nature and organization of the heavenly bodies and the like. There is no reason why a man should not be both a scientist and a philosopher but unless he clearly distinguishes his scientific questions from his philosophical ones, both his science and his philosophy are likely to suffer. Aristotle failed to make this distinction and in this he was followed by nearly all the medieval philosophers.

And so, in the seventeenth century, the physics of Aristotle were not corrected but rather replaced by the physics of Galileo and Newton. Philosophers were henceforth relieved of the duty of trying to solve problems about the observable facts and regularities of nature. But this restriction of their responsibilities was an embarrassment rather than a relief. If all questions of observable fact were questions for the scientist to answer, what questions remained for philosophy and how were they to be approached?

The upshot of the scientific revolution for philosophy is this: Some questions, characteristically those of the natural and social sciences, can be settled by empirical methods, by hypothesis arising out of observation and observation confirming hypothesis. Other questions, characteristic of logical

Philosophy of Education

and mathematical subject matters, can be settled by calculation in accordance with settled rules of deduction. But there are a very large number of questions that do not seem to fall into either of these categories and among these are the traditional problems of philosophy, of ethics and of natural religion. But if such questions cannot be decided either by empirical or by purely deductive methods, how are they to be answered? This is the problem that has been set to philosophy by the success of natural science. Of course, we see it more clearly at the present day than did the philosophers of the seventeenth and eighteenth centuries since we have the advantage of profiting by their work. But it was well understood by most of them that the first problem for the philosopher had become the problem of finding a method. Descartes[1] and Spinoza, impressed by the certainty and efficiency of mathematical methods of proof, tried to prove philosophical conclusions as they proved problems in geometry, and actually set out part of their work in the axiomatic form of Euclid's *Elements of Geometry*. They were unsuccessful, as they misunderstood the nature of the axiomatic method that they were trying to use and overlooked the differences between mathematical symbolism and the language of philosophical arguments. Other philosophers, like Locke[2] and Kant,[3] did not raise the method so directly and preferred to ask: 'What are the limits of human knowledge?' They tried to outline a sort of programme of possible discoveries based upon our knowledge of the powers cf the human mind. Instead of speculating about the nature of the universe and man's place in it, as the Greeks and the medievals had done, they wanted, in Locke's words, first 'to take a survey of our own understandings, examine our own powers and see to what things they were adapted'.

This examination of the powers of the mind proved just as

---

[1] René Descartes (1595–1650), a French mathematician, philosopher and scientist.

[2] John Locke (1632–1704), an English philosopher.

[3] Immanuel Kant (1724–1804) was Professor of Philosophy in Königsberg.

difficult and controversial a matter as any of the traditional problems of philosophy. It served a useful purpose, indeed, in directing the attention of philosophers to what has been called 'the theory of knowledge', a group of important problems concerning the origin, nature and validity of human knowledge. Thus the moderate scepticism of the philosophers who tried in this way to solve the problem of philosophical method achieved only the incidental success of opening up a new field of enquiry. And as long as the problem of method was unsolved, this addition to the field of philosophy was rather like discovering new diseases without finding cures for the old ones. Nevertheless, though Locke's project of finding out the powers and limits of the human mind proved not to be the looked-for philosophical method, questions of this sort do offer a very good starting point for the search for such a method. Let us therefore look more closely at a variant of Locke's question: What kinds of problems can human reason solve for us?

II

Like many of the abstract words used in philosophy, the word 'reason' is a vague one. There is no one 'correct' definition by which we can pin down and fix its meaning. I shall take it to mean the capacity to solve problems, of whatever kind the problem may be; or, to put the same point in another way, reason is the ability to answer questions appropriately. We may defer for the present the obvious queries that arise from this: How do we know when a problem has been solved? How do we know what is an *appropriate* answer? The definition may seem perhaps a rather modest and restricted account of what we mean by 'reason'. But at least there is no doubt that human beings do have such a problem solving capacity as part of their make up. Some of us may have it to a greater degree than others or have a specially good or specially poor capacity for solving some sorts of problems. (For example, those of mathematics or of administration.) But all human beings who are not very low grade mental defectives have this capacity in some degree, sufficient perhaps to justify us being described by the traditional epithet 'rational animals'. And of course, we should remember that the so-called brute animals, dogs, rats and the rest, have their own modest problem-solving capacities. This will remind us that rationality is a matter of degree and not a clear cut 'all or nothing' affair.

We can expect too much of reason or again expect too little of it and it is easy to trace in the history of thought both of these mistaken attitudes. But of the people who have a wrong estimate of the powers of reason, those who over-value it are less at fault than those who despise it. Perhaps the best example of a large body of men who placed an exaggerated value on the powers of human reason is that of the medieval philosophers.

The defects of medieval thinking were not due to lack of talent or of intellectual curiosity. Many medieval philosophers were men of great intellectual gifts and a wide range of interests. What they lacked was a correct conception of what the human mind was capable of knowing and of how it should set about acquiring the knowledge that lay within its power. They were fully convinced that men could prove from ordinary commonsense knowledge plus a few so-called 'self-evident principles' a large number of statements about the existence and nature of God, the nature and destiny of man, the constitution of the physical universe and so on. But unlike proofs in either mathematics or in natural science, their 'proofs' on these subjects have not commanded any general assent among equally competent and well-informed philosophers. That is to say, the metaphysical findings of the medievals do not meet the criteria that we ordinarily apply to the theories offered to the world by scientists, mathematicians, scholars, economists and so on, namely the criteria of independent checking by experts in the same field and coherence with the established body of knowledge in that field. There is indeed no such established body of positive philosophical knowledge: and philosophy being the sort of enterprise that it is, there never could be. Any first-year undergraduate can point out the logical flaws in the scholastic 'proofs' for the existence of God and the immortality of the soul and the like. The reason for the failure of the medieval philosophers seems to have been that they had not openly raised and settled the fundamental question: What kind of evidence would be appropriate to the sort of questions that we are asking? And that they had failed to do this was due not to any intellectual defects on their part but to the historical fact, which has already been noticed above, that they did not have at their command any large body of well-established knowledge which was public, testable and communicable. Such a body of knowledge would have served as a standard of comparison by providing them with at least one reliable example of what organized knowledge really was.

It is much better to trust reason too far than to trust it too little because by trusting it too far we learn through experience where its limits lie. We are thereby better armed for future attempts at solving our problems. We must give the philosophers and theologians of the middle ages the credit for having made for us the experiment of testing human reason beyond its utmost limits and showing, however inadvertently, to their successors where these limits may be found. But there is nevertheless a serious danger in this over-confidence about the powers of reason. If we consistently fail to reach definite and generally accepted results by rational methods, we may well come in time to mistrust the use of reason and to react against it. John Locke, writing in the seventeenth-century reaction against the methods of the medieval scholastics, put this point as follows:

> Thus men extending their enquiries beyond their capacities and letting their thoughts wander into those depths where they can find no sure footing, it is no wonder that they raise questions and multiply disputes, which, never coming to any clear resolution, are proper only to continue and increase their doubts and confirm them at last in perfect scepticism.

The second of the wrong attitudes to reason is the one which undervalues and mistrusts it. This attitude takes two forms, appealing to two quite different types of mind. On the one hand, there is what may be called the born irrationalist. He is the sort of man who shrinks from and distrusts any systematic use of reason. Confronted with a problem that calls for hard and careful thinking, he will either shirk it or turn to bogus substitute methods of solution. The irrationalist will decry what he calls 'intellect' or 'logic' and praise instead mysterious natural impulses and intuitions. It is a very widespread attitude and characterizes the intellectually lazy, the woolly minded, the fanatical and the superstitious. And it is the more pernicious in having supporters who enjoy some reputation—philosophers such as Nietzsche and Bergson, theologians like Kierkegaard and a great many artists and writers, to say nothing of well-known pretentious mystagogues like Rudolf Steiner and Ouspensky. Two contemporary examples of the effect of this attitude can be seen in the psychological theories (if they can so be called) of Carl Jung and the existentialist movement in Europe.

A second and very different type of mind that is prone to undervalue reason is that of the sceptic. The sceptic's distrust of reason arises paradoxically from a limited faith in it. He is prepared to justify and defend his attitude by offering reasons for it, by pointing to the general fallibility of the human mind and the untrustworthiness of all the sources of our knowledge from our senses and memory to our powers of deduction and our so-called intuitions. This is a much more healthy attitude and is indeed an excellent *preliminary* to philosophical thinking. The sceptic, unlike the irrationalist, does not avoid or decry rational processes of thought and behaviour. He merely says that they are of very limited application. And in support of this (for he is rational enough to offer evidence for his statements) he points out that human beings are constantly making mistakes, endorsing and clinging to superstitions, taking dubieties for certainties and generally exhibiting in their behaviour the impotence of reason in action. This evidence that the sceptic offers is true enough but it does not justify his conclusion. If, indeed, we had no reliable standards whatever for distinguishing true statements from false ones and for assessing probabilities with success, the sceptic would be right. But we are not in that unfortunate position and if we were, we could not live successfully in the world at all. We may, perhaps somewhat fancifully, look upon our rational powers as a hand of cards to be played in a game like bridge or poker. To get the best out of them, they must neither be overplayed nor underplayed. We must neither grasp at knowledge that reason cannot ever give us nor ignore what it can successfully offer us. The scholastic metaphysicians (and, less excusably, other metaphysicians since their time) overplayed their hand. The irrationalists and the sceptics underplay it. What we have to do is to recognize what reason is capable of achieving and see that we use it only for those ends. But how are we to ensure that we do this?

It is easy enough to state in a general sort of way what reason and rational action consist in. Bertrand Russell once defined a reasonable or rational man as one who always proportioned the degree of intensity with which he held his various beliefs to the amount of evidence available for each belief. To strive after this degree of rationality is no doubt a counsel of perfection. None of us is so reasonable and most of us are very much less so. Nevertheless, if we are to use reason correctly this should be our aim. The use of reason consists in proportioning the degrees of conviction with which we hold our various beliefs to the strength of the evidence that we have to support them. The abuse of reason consists in holding beliefs on insufficient evidence or holding them with a degree of certainty that the evidence does not justify.

Such irrational conviction may of course be inappropriately weak or inappropriately strong, according as we ignore evidence available to us or presume upon evidence that we do not (and perhaps cannot) possess. But being human, we find that we all are very commonly prone to presuming upon absent evidence and not nearly so commonly prone to the fault of the other extreme, (though we all are ready enough to ignore evidence that conflicts with some habitual or cherished belief).

27

The holding of beliefs on insufficient evidence is superstition. We are not superstitious only when we put our faith in bogus sources of knowledge like astrology. We indulge in superstition every time that we repose a degree of belief in a statement that the evidence for the statement does not justify. A belief in the influence of the stars on human lives is only a gross and extreme form of a fault of which we are all guilty in greater or lesser degrees. Many of our moral, religious and political beliefs are superstitious in this sense; and so indeed are some of our scientific ones.

So far, it may seem that I have done nothing but repeat a number of platitudes well-known to us all, even if we ignore them. A critic may reply: 'Of course, we ought to proportion our beliefs to our evidence. Everyone would agree to that. What people do *not* agree on is what constitutes evidence for different sorts of statement. And that is why men disagree on so many different things. They do not disagree on the principle of using appropriate evidence but on the standards by which we decide *what is evidence for what*. And that is what we would like to see decided.'

This is a fair criticism. But it is not at all easy to give a final answer to the question: What sort of evidence is appropriate to the different sorts of questions that we ask? An important part of the work of philosophers in recent years has dealt with just this problem. And although we see both the question and part of the answer to it far more clearly than was previously seen, it cannot be said that there is yet any final agreement on the point. I do not want to suggest that nothing useful can be said on the matter. It is certain however that anything that can usefully be said will not be so platitudinous as what I have said so far. It is well to remember that in philosophy any statement that is not a truism is controversial. Nevertheless, even a truism may be true. Truisms are often worth reaffirming just because what is obvious to one man is not so to another. What we find 'obvious' depends to a large extent on our training, knowledge and preconceptions.

III

I said above that I was going to take the word 'reason' in the sense of a general capacity for problem solving, whether the problem arose from mathematics, from the natural or social sciences, from situations of everyday life, from philosophical or theological speculation or from any other source whatever. Now we can easily see, if we look at the historical facts referred to briefly at the beginning of this chapter, that men have been very much more successful at some kinds of problem than at others. The problems at which we have been most signally successful have been those of mathematics and those of the natural sciences. The extent to which we can nowadays understand and control the forces of nature is a measure of our success in this field. We have been notably less successful in dealing with questions of morals and politics and with those of metaphysics and religion. And we have been only moderately successful in tackling the problems of the social sciences. But it will not help us to try to use the same methods to deal with the intractable questions of philosophy that have worked so well in enabling us to understand the natural world. Questions of morals and metaphysics are simply not susceptible to this sort of treatment. The hope of a 'scientific' philosophy or 'scientific' morality is quite illusory if we mean by these phrases a philosophy or a morality that relies merely upon the methods of the sciences for its conclusions. We shall see later why this is so.

But we can gain some idea of the right approach to these problems by contrasting the spectacular success of the mathematicians and scientists in their own fields with the notable lack of success of the moralists, metaphysicians and theologians in theirs. If we ask ourselves for the reason why natural science suddenly burst into life in the sixteenth and seventeenth centuries, we can see the answer in the history of the subject. Physics became an independent and rapidly growing branch of learning when physicists discovered the method appropriate to their subject matter. It is indeed a complex historical question

Philosophy of Education

why the realization of the value of the experimental method should have occurred just when and where it did. But there is no doubt that the substitution of observation, experiment and measurement for the speculative methods of the medieval Aristotelians was a turning point in history. Mathematics also, though it has a much older lineage, takes its origin as an independent branch of knowledge from the development of the axiomatic method by the Greek geometers. We can learn this much at least from the successes of scientists and mathematicians that no set of problems is likely to yield its solutions until we find the right method of approaching it. The key to problem-solving of all sorts is first to find the general method of solution for the kind of problem in question. How does this help us here?

A quite superficial acquaintance with the history of philosophy will show us that the general method used by philosophers in the past has been deduction from what appeared to be 'self-evident' premisses. They believed, in other words, that it was possible to *prove* their conclusions about the existence of God, human destiny and the like by methods analogous to those used by mathematicians. The subject matter, to be sure, was very different from that of geometry but they supposed that the truth of their conclusions was guaranteed by the truth of the statements from which their arguments started and the logical validity of their deductions from these statements. This belief that philosophical discovery was essentially a process of proof took a long time to lose its plausibility even though none of the classical metaphysicians ever succeeded in proving anything and even though many of them did nevertheless make important philosophical discoveries. But these discoveries, like Columbus' discovery of America, were the by-product of a mistake. There can be no philosophical proofs because philosophy cannot proceed either by the axiomatic method of mathematics or by the experimental way of the scientist. And there are no other kinds of proof but formal deduction on the one hand and the establishment or refutation of hypotheses on the other. This is not to say that philosophy is not an exercise of reason; for reason does not consist only in giving proofs. But we are forced to conclude that questions which cannot be tackled by the deductive methods of mathematics or the observational and experimental methods of the natural and social sciences need a totally new method of approach. And we can get some sort of a lead to such a new approach by considering that scientists and mathematicians are relatively successful in their enquiries because they have a well-defined method of handling their problems. This means that they know in each case what evidence would settle the question that they are asking and that they usually know also how to set about collecting the evidence. Now this is just what we do not know in many questions relating to philosophy, morals, politics, religion and so on—all those questions that seem perennially controversial because there is no established, agreed and tested method of approaching them. The key question that we must ask as a preliminary to any sort of problem-solving procedure is this: What kind of evidence would have a bearing on this question?

If we have to admit, as well we may, that in some cases we simply do not know what the relevant evidence would be, then we should in all honesty admit that *for us* the question is not a meaningful one. This is a vitally important point for the proper use of reason. If you will consider for a moment some very simple examples of questions, you will see that they always presuppose some sort of knowledge about the answer. In other words, for a question to be a genuine one and capable of being answered, the questioner must have some idea of the terms in which the answer will be given. To take a trivial instance. If I say to someone: 'What's the time?' and he replies 'Tomorrow week' or 'Four yards square', I shall think that either he has misunderstood my question or that he is making a silly joke. I shall know not that the answer is *wrong* but that it is *irrelevant*. I shall know this because in asking questions, we ourselves set the framework within which the answer must fall. For an answer to be right or wrong, it must fall within the framework set by the question. And for a question to be a genuine one, it

31

must have a framework that will determine in advance the
form that the answer must take and the terms in which it will
be made. We have such a framework for a question when we
know the *sort* of evidence that will give us the answer but are
ignorant of *exactly what* the evidence will be.

For this reason it is often said of questions, both scientific
and philosophical, that a question well put is already half
answered or that the secret of success lies in asking the right
questions. Now asking the right questions means, among other
things, putting questions that specify implicitly *the type of
evidence* appropriate to their solution.

A meaningful question cannot be quite neutral as to the
answers it invites. The most precise kind of question would be
one which took the form: 'Which of these two answers is right,
A_1, or A_2?' A vaguer question could be represented as asking:
'Which of these possible answers is right, A_1, A_2 . . . or A_n?'
The larger the number n of possible alternative replies the
more general will be the question. And where a question is so
general as not even to imply a set of alternative answers, it
loses its interrogative function. Thus the answer to a vague or
woolly question is to say: What sort of evidence would you
accept as relevant to the answer? If the questioner cannot tell
you what sort of evidence would be relevant to his answer,
his query is a mere pseudo-question, having the grammatical
form of a question but not its interrogative function. For if the
questioner does not know what sort of evidence would be
relevant to his problem, he is in no position to distinguish a
relevant from an irrelevant answer, still less a true answer
from a false one.

We can propose then as a minimum safeguard against the
abuse of reason the use of the following query whenever we
are confronted with a problem: What kind of evidence would
be relevant to the solution? But it is important to notice that
there are two types of situation in which we might be unable
to meet this challenge by specifying the sort of evidence that
we should accept as relevant. (1) It might merely be that we
personally did not know what kind of evidence would answer

the question for us. (2) It might be that there was not and never could be any such evidence. Let us look at these two cases separately.

1 Suppose that I know nothing of mathematics or of natural science. I may put questions to mathematicians or scientists that they can answer quite easily. For example: How is it known that squaring the circle is impossible? How is it known what the sun is made of? How do we know that the tide will be high at midnight on a certain place on January 1st next year? And so on. The experts could give me the answers easily enough but these answers will necessarily presuppose a certain amount of knowledge if they are to be understood. Unless I know a good deal of mathematics I cannot understand the proof that it is impossible to square the circle. Unless I know a good deal of physics and chemistry, I cannot appreciate the spectroscopic evidence about the composition of the sun. Such questions—indeed, almost any question—may be *relatively* unanswerable, that is to say, unanswerable to those persons who do not have the necessary background of knowledge against which the question acquires a meaning. A question may, then, be a pseudo-question relatively to a given person who has not sufficient relevant knowledge to make the answer *meaningful for him*. (Many of the questions of young children are of this kind.) Such a person can always improve his knowledge if he wants to, with the consequence that questions that were once without meaning for him can subsequently acquire it.

2 But there is another sort of question, if it can so be called, that is not meaningless relatively to a particular set of persons but is meaningless in an absolute sense in that there is no framework of knowledge within which the question has a meaning and nobody can make any generally acceptable reply to the challenge: What sort of evidence would be relevant to the answer? The same point may be put in another way. Many questions can be converted into corresponding statements, (Obviously a question of the form 'Is X Y?' can be converted

to 'X is Y'.) This statement, if it is to convey any information, must have a range of possible evidence that would be accepted as supporting it. If the person who makes the statement has not got the evidence that would establish it, he is acting irrationally in believing it. If, in addition to not possessing the evidence for the statement, he has not the faintest idea what sort of evidence would settle the question, he is making a merely empty statement. Now here we have the possibility of a very serious and dangerous kind of philosophical mistake, the making of statements or the asking of questions that have the outward appearance of genuine statements or questions but which, on examination, do not satisfy the criterion that their genuine counterparts must satisfy—namely, possessing a possible range of evidence that, *were it obtainable*, would verify the statement or answer the question. I say that we have the *possibility of this kind of mistake* for it is a matter of debate whether such errors have occurred in serious philosophizing and a matter of philosophical criticism to identify them. But it is easy enough to point to questions of this sort. Suppose that someone asks: When did time begin? Or: What colour is an atom? An intelligent child or an unsophisticated adult might ask such questions because they seem analogous to questions like: When did the Hundred Years' War begin? Or: What colour is uranium? But they can be asked only because the questioner has not reflected on the subject matter of his question. He has not realized that a query of the form 'When did X begin?' presupposes time in the sense of the existence of a convention for temporal measurement and that it makes no sense to ask such a question about time itself. He has not realized, in the second case, that questions of the form 'What colour is X?' presuppose that X is capable of reflecting light and that it makes no sense to ask the question about something like an atom which is too small to reflect any light. In other words, questions may very well be empty if they are asked by someone ignorant or careless of the meaning of terms contained in his question. Now it is perfectly possible to ask such questions and make the corresponding statements in philosophy without realizing that they are in fact empty of content. Indeed, some philosophers have suggested, perhaps unkindly, that all metaphysical statements and questions are of just this kind. Unfortunately, it is not possible to give any useful general rules that will enable us to proscribe such statements and questions in advance. We have to test each one and pass or fail it on its merits. The point of the question: What sort of evidence would be relevant? is to elucidate what are the logical merits of a given statement or question.

IV

It has become obvious to philosophers in the past fifty years that a great many of the unprofitable controversies of the past can take on a new and enlightening aspect if we look at them from this point of view. The metaphysicians who debated about God, morality, human destiny and so on were assuming that these problems were similar to scientific questions at least in being clear questions about definite matters of fact to which answers were in principle possible. Yet it is obvious from the history of philosophy that equally honest, intelligent and well-informed men may have all the supposedly relevant facts at their disposal and still disagree profoundly about such matters. This indicates that the facts which they supposed to be relevant were not really relevant at all. If they had been, it is incredible that generally acceptable answers on these matters should not by now have been reached. For it is important to notice that facts are never relevant in philosophy in the way that they are in history or in science. Historians and scientists may, and often do, disagree on the way in which the available facts are to be interpreted. But these disagreements can, in principle, always be resolved by the discovery of *further* relevant facts; and no historical or scientific disagreement could outlive the knowledge of *all* the facts, if these were ever obtainable. Yet this can and does happen in metaphysical disputes. It is indeed one sure way by which we may recognize that the dispute is metaphysical.

There are two ways of proceeding from this point. We can

say that questions and statements of this sort to which no generally acceptable evidence seems at all relevant, are simply meaningless or nonsensical, that they are grammatically correct forms of words which carry no meaning whatever of an informative kind. This was the view of the logical positivists, a pre-war school of philosophy which no longer survives in its original hard-shelled form. Under this ruling, only two kinds of statement retain any cognitive meaning, statements of empirical fact that can be confirmed by sensory observation and statements of logic and mathematics that can be checked by calculation. Every other kind of statement is ruled out as lacking any kind of cognitive content. This is clearly a very rough way of dealing with the statements of ethics, politics, religion and criticism of literature and the arts as well as the writings of the metaphysicians. And it shows perhaps a rather cavalier and unsympathetic attitude to matters which have excited men of ability and integrity since the beginning of history.

A more tolerant point of view which is now quite widely accepted among philosophers, may be expressed as follows: 'These statements are certainly misleading in looking grammatically like statements of observable fact. But perhaps we are being misled by their linguistic form. After all, language has many uses and fact-stating is only one of them. Let us consider all the other possible uses of language to see if we can re-interpret such apparently empty propositions in such a way that we can see what they are really asserting and so come to some agreed decision about their value.' This is one of the ways in which modern philosophers have come to be very interested in questions of language. And investigations of this kind have proved very fruitful in putting some of the oldest controversies of philosophy in quite a new light. Unfortunately, it is not easy to give in a summary way any adequate idea of the methods and results of the contemporary linguistic approach to philosophy. A general description of this work would be too vague to be informative. It can be appreciated only by seeing it in action.

All I can usefully do here is to give in illustration one or two of the more important discoveries about language and its workings that have been brought to light by these methods and show how they are philosophically enlightening. Perhaps the most basic of these notions (it is hardly recondite enough to be called a discovery) is a principle which derives chiefly from the work of G. E. Moore:[1] *The meaning of a word is created and controlled by the ways in which it is used.* To say this is merely to say that the relations between a word or phrase and its meaning is not a part of nature independent of human wishes but rests upon social conventions. Words and phrases have those powers of communication that their habitual modes of use have endowed them with, *and no more.* This fact, obvious enough though it is, has important consequences for philosophy.

It follows from this that many words, and among them most of the key terms of philosophy, must be both vague and ambiguous *and irremediably so.* For it is clear that the abstract and uncommon terms of philosophy will be used much less often and in much less concrete contexts than the words describing the common features of our everyday experience. They will thus be much vaguer since the precedents for their use in some contexts will not have been clearly established or, indeed, established at all. And they will be ambiguous when divergent or incompatible speech customs have directed the occasions of their use. The philosopher faced with these natural debilities of language is often in the position of an English judge who has to give a judgment in a common law case for which the relevant precedents are either conflicting or fail to cover the circumstances at issue. But whereas the judge knows that his judgment must contain some arbitrary element, the classical philosopher, blind to the nature of language, too often assumed that he had given the only right answer to his problem.

The modern philosopher who is sensitive to this natural feature of language often looks to the ways in which we remedy

[1] Professor G. E. Moore (1873–   ) was Professor of Philosophy at Cambridge University from 1925 to 1939.

vagueness when it troubles us in everyday speech. We commonly do so by pointing to examples and especially to borderline examples. If someone asks, for instance, 'What colours do you include under the term "violet"?' you can show him a range of samples, both of the shades you are prepared to call 'violet' and also of those that are just too red or too blue to qualify for the term. Procedures of this kind will make your meaning much more precise, though still not perfectly so. In philosophy, the vagueness of such terms as 'mind', 'thought', 'God', 'free will', 'cause' or 'substance' is not so easily treated by this method. But where we can do something on these lines, the consequences may be important.

To take a concrete case, if we ask: 'What do you mean by "thinking"?', you might give a series of examples: I am thinking when I am daydreaming, when I am doing mathematics, when I am writing a letter, when I am playing chess, when I am talking with friends and so on. But are you thinking when you are dreaming as well as when you are daydreaming, when you are batting at cricket, as well as when you are playing chess, when you are playing the piano as well as when you are solving equations? And if you are thinking when you are solving your puzzles, does the rat think when he is solving his? Examples and counter-examples of this sort show how fuzzy this and similar concepts are round their edges and how there are no standard examples of them with a unitary set of properties that all genuine instances of the concept possess. Thinking is not an all-or-none affair but a matter of degree; and so too with the rest of those philosophical concepts whose vagueness can be elucidated in this way. The result of the elucidation is to show that these concepts are in no way like precise clear-cut technical terms. Thus a consideration of the workings of language has thrown new light on the nature of a concept and has gone a long way towards disposing of a philosophical problem that has been outstanding since Plato.

There is another important application of this principle that offers a useful way of deciding some philosophical questions. It has been called by a contemporary philosopher, Professor

J. O. Urmson, the 'appeal to the standard example'. He instances a well-known application of this method by Susan Stebbing in her critique of Eddington in *Philosophy and the Physicists*. In *The Nature of the Physical World*, his popular exposition of twentieth-century advances in physics, Eddington tried to explain the scientist's view of material objects as follows. Solid objects, like tables and stones, were not really solid or substantial at all for the physicists had shown them to be clouds of tiny particles separated by distances that were very large in relation to the size of the particles. The floor that we tread upon, Eddington explained, was really much more like a swarm of flies than a plank of wood and had, as he put it, 'no solidity of substance'. It was really very remarkable that it supported the weight of anything placed upon it.

This piece of amateur philosophizing was decisively refuted by Stebbing in the following way. She pointed out that the word 'solid' takes its meaning from its application to things like stones and tables and planks. If they are not solid, then nothing is, for it is by reference to such things that we learn to use the word 'solid'. If the word has no application to the standard cases of its use, it loses its meaning and has, in consequence, no application at all. Stebbing thus showed in this simple way that the language in which Eddington tried to explain physical discoveries, far from being enlightening, was simply misleading. This kind of appeal to the standard uses of words has had very wide application in contemporary philosophy and has proved a very effective logical weapon. It is particularly powerful in exposing the emptiness of those metaphysical theories whose point depends upon using ordinary words in very extraordinary senses. The well-known 'first cause' argument[1] for the existence of God is an example of this sort.

A secondary important discovery about language that is philosophically important is that language is not a picture or

[1] This argument, which purports to prove a 'first cause' of the whole universe, uses the word 'cause' in a sense entirely different from that conferred on it by ordinary usage.

map of the world and, in consequence, no conclusions can be drawn from the nature of language to the nature of reality. This is a very large subject, and in its details, still a controversial one. But briefly the position is that many of the classical philosophers assumed that our thinking about the world mirrored what we found there, at least when our thinking was not mistaken and that our language mirrored our thinking. It was believed that thinking, correct or mistaken, was a sort of mapping of the universe and that the map was a good one when our thinking was true and a bad or distorted or even totally misleading one when our beliefs were false. Moreover, language was a sort of externalized model of our internal cogitations, the map, as it were, in its published form. This view was first stated in an embryonic form by Aristotle and was later canonized into what was called the Correspondence Theory of Truth. There is just enough in this kind of metaphor to make it easy for us to press it too far. The real harm of this three-level view of knowledge, thinking mirroring fact and language mirroring thinking, is not so much in the metaphor of the mirror or the map, though this is a misleading way of explaining even very elementary kinds of knowledge. The danger lies rather in the supposed split between thinking and its expression as if thinking is some sort of mysterious inner process that can proceed apart from language or from any other kind of symbolism whatever. Both the sources of this error and its consequences are too complicated to dwell on here. One of its most damaging results is to make us suppose that the actual grammatical and syntactical structures of natural languages are a key to the nature of reality. For language, on this view, is a picture of the world, or rather, a picture of a picture. And what we find in the structure of languages may fairly be supposed to correspond to the structure of the world. Thus to take one example, some metaphysicians seem to have taken the grammatical distinction between subject and predicate as evidence for the philosophical theory that the world consisted of a number of substances characterized by different properties.

V

Let us consider how these views about language bear upon the work of the classical metaphysicians. We have seen that these philosophers, like contemporary philosophers, dealt with such questions as the following: What is the nature of the connexion between the private 'mental' events that occur in our consciousness and the physical events that occur in our sense organs and nervous systems? Are all mental events, including our choices, effects which can be completely explained and in principle predicted by an adequate knowledge of preceding events? What is the nature of the mind or self? That is to say, can we give an adequate account of it in terms of mental events or nervous events or both, or do we have to explain the facts of our mental life by supposing an unknown immaterial something which we can never experience but which we must postulate to make our experience logically coherent? What is the nature of the objects revealed to us by the senses? That is to say, how are we to describe them in order to allow for all the facts of normal and abnormal sense experience?

These particular philosophical questions look superficially like the problems of the psychologist because they deal with the subject matter of psychology. But they are not questions that can ever be answered by the psychologist as a scientist because no amount of factual evidence collected by the most careful observation and experiment could ever finally settle them. Now when the classical philosophers were faced with problems of this kind they were not bothered by the fact that observational evidence was not relevant to their solution. They assumed that as philosophers they had special methods of dealing with such problems which were perfectly logical and efficient although they were not the methods of natural science. We have seen that these supposedly philosophical methods of the classical philosophers have fallen into disrepute in recent years simply because they do not give the results that they promise. No alleged solution of any philosophical problem achieved by these methods has ever satisfied more than a small minority of philosophers. But our present interest in them is to see how they are connected with the mistakes about language discussed above. Such solutions usually consisted in showing how a certain view about the relation between mind and body, for example, followed as a logical consequence of a certain metaphysical system. These metaphysical systems were very general world pictures or, as it were, charts of the universe which were supposed to be established by a logical process of argument from statements which everyone would admit to be self-evidently true. And if we look at the methods of the philosophers who tried to work out such systems, it is easy to see why an examination of the powers and functions of language was a vital preliminary to their enterprise. They were trying to do for the universe as a whole what the natural scientists do for limited portions or aspects of the universe. They were trying to give a general ordered account of everything that exists in terms of abstract notions like existence, cause, substance, quality, space, time, matter, mind and so on just as the physicist gives such an account of certain aspects of the physical world in terms of energy, mass, velocity and so on. But it is important to notice that the similarities between metaphysics and natural science are superficial and delusive while the differences between them are fundamental. There are two principal differences. In the first place, the physicists' theories about the world are based on controlled and accurate observation and can be checked by further observation. And if found substantially correct, they can be embodied in useful gadgets like dynamos and refrigerators which will be found to work efficiently. But the metaphysicians' theories about the world are never of this kind. No observations are relevant to the suggestions that time is unreal or that essence and existence are identical in God or that the human mind is immaterial. Nor can such suggestions be put to any practical use.

This, of itself, is no fatal criticism. But if these theories can neither be confirmed or refuted by observation, how are they to be established? This question points to a second difference between metaphysics and science. The metaphysician, unlike the scientist, derives his theories by tracing the logical connexions between statements expressed in ordinary language enriched by the technical terms of his philosophical vocabulary. And by such tracing of logical connexions, he claims to find out new, exciting and often paradoxical facts about the universe and man's relation to it. Now it is obvious that this procedure implies a great faith in the symbolic powers of ordinary language. It is true that mathematicians can make new and surprising discoveries by tracing the logical connexions between symbolic expressions. But the symbols of mathematics are carefully and exactly defined and are totally different in nature and function from the words of our natural languages. Nor do the results of mathematics, *before they have been applied to the world*, yield us any new facts about the world. No one can trace the first beginnings of the systems of signs that make up our natural languages like English and French but it is not unreasonable to suppose that in their early stages they were developed to express everyday emotions and communicate facts of common interest in a primitive society. The development of the abstract vocabulary that philosophers need is a very late stage in all languages and there are many languages at the present day which would be useless as media for philosophical writing merely because philosophical activities are not represented in the cultures in which these languages have developed.

The metaphysician has an answer to this charge of blind confidence in the symbolic powers of language. He would probably say something like this: 'You are confusing the issue in stressing the limitations of language. All of us use language, whether in writing philosophy or in teatime gossip, only to express our thoughts. And though it is true that where thinking becomes very complex or abstract, the limitations of language act as a check on our *powers of expression*, they do not prevent us from thinking. Where we have no words adequate to express our thoughts, we invent new ones which are designed to express them. If this were not so, the civilized languages would never have developed from the uncouth dialects of illiterate peoples.

In short, we think first and then clothe our thoughts in language. And when we do metaphysics and try to discover the general nature of the universe, we are relying not on tracing the logical connexions between one linguistic expression and another but in tracing those connexions between one thought or judgment and another. And because these judgments are judgments about reality, their logical consequences will give us new and often unexpected information about the universe we live in and our relation to it.' If metaphysicians wish to defend their traditional methods they will be forced to reply to the charge of linguistic innocence outlined above in something like these terms. (Indeed, this sort of defence has been offered by some of them.) But it will be seen that this reply rests on the very assumptions about language that recently have been called in question: (1) that thinking is a process prior to and independent of language or any other kind of symbolization; (2) that words can have meanings that are to some degree independent of the way in which they are used. And there is very good reason to suppose that both these assumptions are false. If we consider the second assumption, in particular, it will be obvious that unless we believe that words have 'natural meanings' independent of the contexts in which they have been used, abstract concepts of philosophy are far too vague and fluid to enable us to trace any logical connexion between them that will enable us to make discoveries about reality. Philosophers who used this method have in fact been forced to supplement the inadequacies of conventional rules of usage by supplying rules of their own in the form of *definitions* of their basic terms. But, of course, no new information about the universe could ever be extracted from definitions.

I do not wish to suggest that traditional metaphysics must be rejected merely because of recent philosophical views about language. These views do indeed bring into focus some of the *reasons* for the failure of metaphysical speculation but the failure was obvious long before the attention of modern philosophers was directed to the nature of language. I suggested at the beginning of this chapter that no system of traditional metaphysics has ever proved to be publicly testable by experts in the same field and coherent with the rest of established knowledge; and that this, in itself, refuted the claims of such systems to be taken seriously. If it is objected that this is an unfair criterion to use because it has been developed by application to factual disciplines like science and history, we have to ask: How else is the truth of any theory, historical, scientific, mathematical or philosophical, to be established? We learn to recognize truth in the future by seeing how it has come to be recognized in the past. Public recognition by experts, progressive corrigibility and coherence with established knowledge are not indeed *infallible* guarantees of true beliefs. For truth has no such hall marks. But they are the best guarantees we have. And it would be absurd to accept any belief which lacked them as more than a tentative hypothesis. We cannot indeed even regard it as a hypothesis unless we know (*a*) what consequences would follow if it were true; and (*b*) how these consequences are to be established.[1] The basic weakness of metaphysics has been that its practitioners claimed objective truth for their conclusions without recognizing objective tests by which their claim could be verified.

No doubt there will be metaphysical systems in the future which will take account of the way in which language works and even of the need for criteria of proof. Such systems will have to be judged on their merits. But the present state of philosophical knowledge and its past history cannot encourage us to look on philosophy as more than a laborious piecemeal effort to criticize and clarify the foundations of our beliefs. Such successes as philosophers can claim have all been of this kind. And this means that in the present condition of human knowledge we cannot hope for more from philosophy than occasional and fragmentary glimpses of enlightenment along with a reasonable confidence that its continuous practice will keep our minds free of nonsense. But this is something very valuable that only philosophy can give us.

[1] See Chapter 4 for a discussion of this point.

45

3

THE JUSTIFICATION OF VALUE JUDGMENTS

I

IT has been regarded as the proper concern of a philosopher to explain, criticize or even justify moral standards and the judgments that are made in accordance with such standards. The work of moral philosophers in the past has commonly had a practical aim. They expected that their enquiries into the nature of moral judgments would enable us to answer the question 'What is the right way to live?' with greater and more justified assurance than we did before. At the present time, moral philosophers are very much more cautious in making claims of this kind and in arousing such expectations in their readers. There are good reasons for their diffidence. One practical reason, as we have seen, is that none of the attempts of their predecessors has been successful in commanding more than a very limited assent and that they have all proved vulnerable to criticism. But there is an even better reason of a theoretical kind for distrusting the claims of philosophers to be able to provide moral guidance. We can now see, in the light of the work of previous philosophers, that it is logically absurd to suppose that a practical conclusion about what we are morally obliged to do could ever be *demonstrated*. I shall return to this point later.

It is however curious that this modesty on the part of contemporary philosophers is not well received by the intelligent layman who feels that he has the right to expect from the philosopher a rational exposition of 'the meaning of existence' or of 'the purpose of life'. This is a very odd demand. No layman would think of requesting that a scientist should produce a perpetual motion machine or an elixir of life merely on the grounds that it would be desirable to have such a thing and that scientists in the past have made ill-founded claims to have discovered these marvels. And it would be a particularly odd request if the layman persisted in making it in the face of the scientists' assurances that there were good technical reasons for supposing that these feats were impossible. Yet the demand of the layman to have 'the purpose of life' demonstrated to him is precisely analogous to this. Philosophers have claimed in the past to be able to provide such knowledge and have had their claims refuted. And there are good reasons of a logical kind for saying that such knowledge is, in principle, beyond the reach of any philosophical argument. No doubt philosophers should blame the pretensions of their predecessors for the fact that they are faced with these embarrassing demands. However that may be, the discipline of philosophy can offer something valuable to the man who wants to know 'the meaning of existence'.[1] He can be shown how to apply the touchstone of critical analysis to the many varied answers that have been given to his questions and, more importantly, to the questions themselves. By enabling him to know what he is looking for, philosophy can help him to see where he can find it, if it can be found at all.

It is after all a commonplace that the first step to wisdom lies in realizing our own ignorance and incapacities. Let us start by looking at the way in which disputes about moral values can arise. It is clear that nearly all human beings have opinions about right and wrong in conduct. They agree that certain sorts of conduct should be approved and encouraged and certain other sorts of conduct condemned and discouraged. But they tend nevertheless to disagree on two points: (*a*) on what kinds of conduct should be approved and condemned;

[1] See Chapter 6 below.

47

(*b*) on *why* approval ought to be given to morally acceptable conduct and conversely, *why* wrong conduct is said to be wrong. That is to say, there is no agreement on what moral rules ought to be followed nor on what principles such moral rules are accepted. An example of the first kind of disagreement would be a disagreement between two people one of whom held that suicide, for example, or divorce or birth control was always morally wrong and the other held that it was sometimes morally permitted or even obligatory. An example of the second kind of disagreement would arise if two men agreed that a certain sort of conduct was always morally wrong but disagreed on *why* it was wrong. One of them might hold that it was wrong because it contravened a moral law laid down by God and because it was always a part of man's duty to obey God's laws. The other might say that such conduct was wrong because it tended, on the whole and in the long run, to lessen the amount of happiness in the world and that it was an overriding moral rule always so to act as to maximize human happiness.

Both these sorts of disagreement are worth examining more closely. Let us look at the first one. We see here that people agree that words like 'good' and 'bad', 'right' and 'wrong' have both a meaning and a proper application when used to refer to human conduct just as they agree that words like 'red' and 'yellow', 'sweet' and 'sour' have a meaning and a proper application in describing our experiences of seeing and tasting. Nevertheless, though they agree that these moral words have both a meaning and a field of application, they may disagree strongly both as to the meaning of such words and as to the correct way in which they are to be applied.

It should be noticed that in the case of everyday descriptive words there is usually no separation between the meaning (or connotation) of a word and its field of application (or denotation). This is so because we first learn the meanings of such words by seeing how they are applied and later learn to apply other words by finding out their meanings. Some words, it is true, have a meaning without having any field of application.

The word 'dragon', for example, means 'a large winged fire-breathing reptile' but does not *refer* to anything in the universe, for such things do not exist. Conversely a proper name like 'Tray' may be used to *refer to* a certain dog but cannot properly be said to have a *meaning*. But with the vast majority of ordinary words, meaning and field of application go together. That is why it is very puzzling when we find divergences between them as we seem to do in the case of value words. For two people may agree (or appear to agree) on the meaning of the word 'wrong' for example, without agreeing very closely on its proper field of application. Suppose, for example, two men who agreed that wrong actions were those that tended to lower the level of human happiness but disagreed on whether the practice of birth control had this effect. Again, more strangely still, they might disagree on the meaning of the word 'wrong' while agreeing on how it should be applied. An instance of this kind would occur if two men agreed that suicide, for example, was wrong but one of them held it to be wrong because it contravened a divine edict while the other held that its wrongness lay in its tendency to reduce the level of human happiness.

I remarked above that disagreements of this kind do not often occur about the meaning and application of those words that relate to sense experience. Indeed, in the case of simple sense qualities like 'blue' or 'sweet' the meaning of the word is learned by observing the instances to which it is applied. Thus the criteria by which the meanings of such words are determined are the very occasions on which they are applied. In such cases, therefore, it is *logically* impossible to separate meaning and application so as to agree on one and disagree on the other. And where such disagreements arise in the case of more complex qualities, we have ways of resolving them. Two people, without any specialized knowledge of biology, might dispute whether a whale was a fish. In this instance, the dispute would concern either the meaning or the application of a word and it could therefore arise in one of two ways. A and B might agree as to the characters an animal had to possess in order to be called a fish (that is to say, they might agree on the meaning of 'fish') but disagree on the factual question of whether or not the whale possessed these defining characters. Or alternatively, A and B might agree on the purely factual issue of the structure of whales but disagree on the *verbal* issue of whether or not the word 'fish' was properly applied to creatures with this structure.

But in both of these sorts of argument, we know how to settle the issue. If we are agreed on the *meaning* of a word but disagree on its *application*, all we have to do is to examine the observable properties of the thing over which the disagreement has arisen; in the case of the whale, once we have determined by observation that the whale is a warm-blooded creature with a four-chambered heart, breathing by means of lungs and suckling its young, we know that this does not satisfy the criteria laid down in the accepted zoologists' definition of 'fish'. But if we agree that the whale has these properties but claim nevertheless that it should be called a fish because it is shaped rather like one and lives in the sea, then our dispute is one about the meaning of the word 'fish'. This kind of dispute is not so indubitably a factual matter and cannot always be settled quite so easily.

If there is a generally accepted definition of the word in question or a generally established way of using it, we point to this definition or to this common usage and to the further fact that meanings are (and can only be) established by common usage in this way. But if the definition is a vague one, disputes may easily arise as to whether the case in question satisfied the definition. This may often happen; for no definition or usage can be perfectly precise. For example, we might argue whether or not a virus is to be regarded as a living organism when it behaves in solution like an organism and in crystalline form like an inorganic substance. This particular dispute would indeed be a pointless one since it continues after we have all the evidence that would ever be relevant to settling it. It is, in any case, of no practical importance to the scientist in his dealings with viruses. But questions of this kind often arise in courts of law, where the matter *is* often of practical importance, for example, to the administration of a will or of an act of parliament. To take examples that have been discussed in the courts: 'Is a sea-plane a *boat*?' 'Are stocks and shares *money*?' 'Is the money I make by backing horses *income*?' There is no incontrovertible way of settling such questions when they arise for the first time and the judge's decision, though based on previous similar cases, must always contain an arbitrary element.

Let us look again in the light of this discussion at the ethical disputes mentioned above. Here we have, apparently, the same sources of disagreement, namely, uncertainty about the meaning of ethical terms and about their field of application. In the case of empirical terms, we have, as we have seen, established procedures for settling disputes of this kind. Where they cannot be decided because of the vagueness of the term whose application is in question, we can see quite clearly why the disputants must agree to differ. But there are no such easy ways of deciding ethical issues or indeed any other disputes about valuations; and there is certainly no willingness on the part of the disputants to agree to differ. In the examples given, where the parties to the dispute profess to agree on the meaning of an ethical term and yet disagree on its application, no scrutiny of the facts of the case will settle the question except perhaps where both parties agree that 'right' and 'wrong' are definable in terms of the observable consequences of an action. (This is no doubt one reason why such 'utilitarian' theories of ethics have always been in favour with empirically minded philosophers.) If the dispute is about the meaning of an ethical term rather than its application, here again the methods effective in empirical disputes will not settle the argument. This is because (*a*) the conventional usages that govern the meaning of ethical terms are not perfectly definite; and (*b*) even if we could point to such a usage, it would not persuade our opponent who might simply reply that the usage, however general, was simply misguided. (Such a reply would not, of course, even make sense with reference to the meaning of an ordinary empirical term like 'blue', 'dog' or 'large'.) Let us suppose, for example, a Christian missionary who is trying to convert a community of utilitarians. However uniformly the word 'wrong' was used in such a community in the sense of 'tending to diminish human happiness', the Christian might still wish to contend that the word 'wrong' *really* meant 'contravening the divine law'. It is, to be sure, not at all clear what such a use of the phrase '*really* means' would be claiming in this dispute. For it is certainly not like the case of the chemist who tells us that air is *really* a mixture and not an element or a compound. But the very fact that the claim can be made at all shows how very different the ethical dispute is from the kinds of empirical dispute that we naturally tend to suppose are analogous to it. And it is these features of ethical disputes (and others like them) that make them problems for the philosopher.

II

These problems of moral philosophy are closely relevant to education in the wide sense in which we have agreed to take the word. What can be taken as a good for the educator will fall into one of two classes. It may be good in the instrumental sense of the word, that is to say, good as a means to a given end. Thus a certain type of school organization or a certain technique of teaching might be considered good in this sense and the fact that it was adopted would be evidence that it was *considered* instrumentally good by the authorities who adopted it. For example, the organization of comprehensive schools may be considered an efficient means of bringing about new social attitudes in parents and children. These new social attitudes may in turn be believed to be good in the instrumental sense, that is, efficient means to some further end, such as perhaps the furthering of a classless society. This last end may in turn be thought to be essential to a happy society. But presumably the production of a happy society would be believed to be good not as a means to anything else, but simply as good in itself. Of course, the judgment that a particular instrumental good will bring about its intended object may well be mistaken. Perhaps it may turn out that comprehensive schools do not bring about the new social attitudes expected of them or that the classless society, when it arrives, will not produce the happy effects anticipated or will not be unique in doing this. But these mistakes, if they occurred, would be mistakes of *fact* occurring in the fields of sociology and political science. They would not be philosophical errors. For the philosopher would be concerned only with the criticism and clarification of the value judgments that direct these policies, that is to say, the judgments that specify what things are good in themselves or good *as ends*.

This commonplace distinction[1] between things that are good as means and those that are good as ends is important in any theoretical discussion of human action, whether in the field of morals, politics, economics or education. One point that is worth emphasizing here is this: The question 'Is X good?' where 'good' is used in the instrumental sense, can fairly be translated: 'Is X an efficient means of obtaining Y?' 'Is this a good knife?' means 'Does this cut well?' 'Is this a good car?' means 'Does it run smoothly, reliably and economically?' and so on. In such contexts, 'good' means no more than 'successful' or 'efficient'. Now questions like these are *questions of empirical fact* that can be settled by observation, experiment, testimony or, in a word, by *experience*. It follows, as I said above, that philosophy can give no help with questions of this kind, apart perhaps from showing on occasions that a given empirical question is in fact empirical. (This is not always so obvious that it calls for no remark.)

Where such questions are not matters of commonsense observation, they are matters for the scientist who is an expert in the appropriate field. If we ask whether some given technique of teaching or administration is good in this sense, we need first to ask: (*a*) What is it supposed to do? (*b*) Is it successful in

---

[1] It will be obvious that this discussion seriously oversimplifies the very complex relations between ends and means. It is misleading to make the distinction between them sharp and absolute if only because many things are good as means and also valued for their own sakes. But with this warning about the complexity of the issue, the commonsense distinction used above is a very useful one in elementary discussions.

effecting this? It is well to remember that we cannot possibly answer questions of this kind without first having answers to both (a) and (b). Moreover, the answer to (b) is very often, in educational questions, a matter of expert evaluation of complex statistical evidence. The question cannot therefore be finally settled as long as the evidence is incomplete, nor can it be settled by anyone who is not an expert in assessing such evidence. An excellent example of the difficulties met with in assessing the instrumental value of a proposed educational reform was given by the controversy in Britain after the second world war about the age of transfer from primary to secondary schools. The expert findings of the psychologists were not entirely unanimous on the matter but there was a substantial balance of opinion that the most educationally efficient age for the change was at twelve or thirteen.[1] But against this majority opinion, it was necessary to weigh the considerable administrative problems of altering the balance between primary and secondary education in this way and the educational consequences of transferring children to a grammar school curriculum a year or two later than had previously been the practice. In the event, the advantages of the *status quo* seem to have been thought to outweigh the rival advantages to be expected from a change in the age of transfer. Here we have a case where the factual evidence for a proposed educational change had been determined with a reasonable degree of probability by a consensus of expert opinion. The administrators in charge of educational policy had then to make a choice between rival advantages. Educational policy, like economic policy, is usually a matter of estimating the most efficient use to be made of scarce resources—time, buildings, intelligence, teaching skill and so on. The important point to remember in all such cases is that where something proposed as an educational advance or reform is recommended, as it usually is, on the ground that it is a means to some socially accepted end, the

[1] See Burt: *British Journal of Educational Psychology* (Vol. XIII, 1943) and *Age, Ability and Aptitude* in University of London Institute of Education Studies in Education No. 6.

proposal is an empirical matter which stands or falls by the evidence that can be adduced in its favour.[1]

If then we grant that the solution of questions about what is good as means is a matter to be settled by observation and experiment, we can hand over such questions to the appropriate experts and await their verdict. But what are we to say of the question: '*How are we to find out what things are good as ends?*' Such questions are not to be decided simply by collecting and assessing evidence. Yet because people may disagree sharply on such issues the question can be a practical as well as a theoretical one. It is of little use that we agree to decide disputes about instrumental goods by an objective assessment of the evidence if we have not agreed on the ends to which these means are to be used. If A and B are driving a car from London to Manchester, they can settle a dispute about the quickest route by consulting a road map. But any such discussion of ways and means will be premature or pointless if A wishes to go to Manchester and B to Land's End.

It is clear then that *questions of value* about what is intrinsically good or about moral obligations or the moral rules or standards that determine such obligations are not questions that can be *finally* answered by the collection and assessment of factual evidence. We must indeed take account of all the facts that may be relevant; but these facts, though they may be necessary to resolve such a dispute, are not usually sufficient. Nor, still more obviously, can such questions be settled by the deductive procedures of mathematics or formal logic. Statements about values are thus at the same time of the first practical importance in directing our actions and policies and yet philosophically puzzling in having no obvious or agreed way in which they can be verified or refuted. This seems a serious problem. For there can be little point in knowing the right way to our destination if we have no means of knowing whether the destination itself is the right one. We may find

[1] This elementary truth of logic is often ignored in educational controversies as the current dispute about comprehensive schools so clearly shows.

later that this is a misleading way of putting our difficulty, but it will do for the present as a pointer to direct discussion.

III

Although there is no obvious and agreed way of confirming or refuting statements about values, we can get some idea of how to approach this question by looking at the ways in which such statements are both like and unlike statements that we *do* know how to verify. We may agree that value statements are not to be proved by the same sort of procedure that we use to prove statements that are unmistakably factual. Nevertheless there are ways in which value statements do resemble statements of fact, and if we are to give a fair account of them, we must not neglect these resemblances. The most obvious of them is that value statements are most naturally expressed in the same linguistic form as similar statements of fact. The moral judgment 'suicide is wicked' is similar to the factual judgment 'suicide is illegal'. The aesthetic judgment 'Beethoven's seventh symphony is a great work' is *grammatically* the same kind of statement as the factual statement 'Beethoven's seventh symphony is written in the key of A major'. What may we conclude from this? It seems reasonable to say that because our ordinary judgments about values, like our ordinary judgments about facts, are most naturally expressed in similar language forms, they make the same sort of claim about their subject matter, namely, that the property that they attribute to the action or the work of art or whatever it may be is an objective one. In other words, we are claiming that moral or aesthetic properties like 'good', 'wrong', 'obligatory', 'beautiful' and so on exist in their own right, and independently of the opinions either of the person who makes the judgment or of anyone else. (Views of this kind are often called *objective* or *objectivist* theories of value.)

Naturally, a person who claims that 'good' and 'right' are objective properties of actions just as 'red' and 'square' are objective properties of things does not rest his case only on the usual grammatical form of our moral judgments. That, of

itself, proves nothing. For such clearly subjective expressions
of taste as 'Ice cream is nice' and 'Oysters are unpleasant' have
the same linguistic form as 'Ice cream is nutritious' or 'Oysters
are rich in iodine'. But whereas we should agree that if I say
'Ice cream is nice', this is often just another way of saying 'I
like ice cream',[1] we should certainly not all agree that 'Suicide
is wrong' can just as well be expressed as 'I disapprove of
suicide'. On the contrary, the point of framing our moral
judgments in this fact-stating way, is to claim that they are, in
some sense or other, objective and independent of our own
preferences or of anybody else's. And that we do make such a
claim is quite conclusively shown by the fact that we argue (and
do not merely disagree) about matters of morals while we do
not argue (though we certainly disagree) about matters of taste
in food.

We have therefore to take seriously the claim that moral
judgments are objective statements of fact. If however we
scrutinize it more closely, there are good reasons to doubt if it
can be defended without serious qualifications. Those philosophers who have maintained objective theories of morals have,
in general, supported their position in one of two ways. (*a*)
Sometimes they have tried to *deduce* statements about our
duties or about the ultimate good from statements of a scientific
kind about the nature of man or from metaphysical statements
about the nature of God or the relations of God to man.
(*b*) Often however they have claimed to have direct *intuitions*
or, in a metaphorical sense of the word, *perceptions* of values.
To mark the fact that such intuitions or perceptions were not
directed to ordinary qualities or relations, philosophers of this
school have sometimes called the objects of their intuitions
'non-natural' qualities. Just as I perceive directly that this rose
is *red* or this book is *on top of* that one, so I perceive that a
certain action is *my duty* or a certain state of affairs is *good* or,
perhaps, that a certain work of art is *beautiful*. The action, the

[1] Though commonly it may mean: 'I like ice cream and most
other people do too'. But this sense is obviously not purely
subjective.

state of affairs and the work of art have respectively the 'non-natural' qualities of being obligatory, being good and being beautiful.

But whether the objectivists have argued for (*a*) or for (*b*), they have in each case met with fatal criticisms. The refutation of (*a*) was first clearly given in 1739 by David Hume in a famous passage of his *Treatise on Human Nature*.[1]

> In every system of morality, which I have hitherto met with, I have always remarked that the author proceeds for some time in the ordinary way of reasoning, and establishes the being of a God, or makes observations concerning human affairs; when of a sudden I am surprised to find that, instead of the usual copulations of propositions, *is* and *is not*, I meet with no proposition that is not connected with an *ought* or an *ought not*. This change is imperceptible; but is, however, of the last consequence. For as this *ought* or *ought not* expresses some new relation or affirmation, it is necessary that it should be observed and explained; and at the same time that a reason should be given for what seems altogether inconceivable, how this new relation can be a deduction from others that are entirely different from it.

Hume's point is a logical one and may be rather crudely illustrated in the following way. Using statements (*A*) and (*B*) below as premisses:

(*A*) All mammals are warm-blooded
(*B*) All mammals have four-chambered hearts

we may validly deduce:

(*C*) Some creatures with four-chambered hearts are warm blooded.

We may *not* validly deduce:

(*D*) Some creatures with four-chambered hearts are warm-blooded and furry.

[1] Book III, Part I, Section i.

For although we know (*D*) to be true, it does not follow from (*A*) and (*B*) since we have introduced into the conclusion the concept 'furry' which does not appear in the premisses. Similarly Hume complains that many philosophers have introduced 'ought' and 'ought not' into the conclusions of their arguments when these concepts do not appear in the premisses. His criticism is a complete refutation of all theories of morals which try to base duties and obligations on the will of God or the nature of man or the relation of man to God and so on. For if these theories contain the notion of obligation in their premisses, the argument is unnecessary and if it is not contained there, the argument is invalid.

Conscious of the force of this criticism, many philosophers since Hume's day have preferred to rest their defence of the objectivity of moral values on appeals to intuition. Seeing that moral values cannot be proved by deductive arguments, they have claimed to find them directly in experience. In the words of John Donne, 'Good is as visible as green' and indeed we come to know it in much the same way. But there is a fatal objection to this alternative also. If everyone agreed on these supposed intuitions of 'non-natural' properties, good, beautiful and the like, the claim would be easier to maintain. But we do not agree on them or even agree that we have such intuitions. To this, the objectivist might reply that the parallel with sensory qualities, colours, sounds and so on still holds; for we sometimes disagree on those as well and account for differences of opinions in terms of colour blindness or tone deafness. And where people lack such experiences altogether we call them blind or deaf. But this answer will not save the theory of moral intuitions. For when we disagree on sensory qualities, we have objective tests for deciding the issue. If Jones and Smith disagree whether a room is warm or cold, they have in the thermometer reading an objective standard of appeal. If they disagree in their judgments of colour, they can appeal to the spectroscope; and so on. But not only are there no such objective tests for checking our supposed intuitions of values; on the theory we are considering there never could be.

In sensory judgments, we can agree to differ in our immediate personal reactions just because we have public tests to which we can appeal from the conflicting deliverances of our senses. But a defender of moral intuitions has no such objective tests to which he can refer conflicting moral judgments. Moreover, he cannot, in the nature of the case, admit such tests without conceding the whole point of his theory. For if he did admit them, the real evidence would lie in the tests by which we corrected our intuitions and not in the intuitions themselves.[1]

Moreover, granted that we do make such claims to objectivity by our moral judgments, may we not be deceiving ourselves? Perhaps we are going too far in trying to assimilate our value judgments to statements of fact. For we can do so only if we neglect equally important resemblances between value statements and *subjective* statements of preference like 'Cricket is the best summer game' or 'Beer is my favourite drink'. Some philosophers have pointed out that we often hear children arguing about matters of taste as if they were demonstrable matters of fact. 'Marmalade's nice.' 'No it's not. It's horrid.' 'No, it isn't.' 'Yes, it is.'—and so on. Though this sort of thing may seem absurd to us, we are not always free from it ourselves. How often are our ostensibly reasoned arguments about politics or religion no more than rationalized versions of unarguable prejudices or preferences? As we grow more sophisticated about these matters, we learn to distinguish genuine statements of fact from those expressions of taste or personal preference that are disguised as objective claims by their grammatical form. And the subjectivist will point out that we come to do this by learning which of these statements can be demonstrated to the public satisfaction by adducing evidence and which cannot. If we look at the three statements:

(*A*) Cruelty to animals is punishable by law
(*B*) Cruelty to animals is horrible
(*C*) Cruelty to animals is morally wrong

[1] For an excellent discussion of this point, see P. H. Nowell Smith's *Ethics*, Chapter 3.

we can all agree that (*A*) is a statement of fact that can be checked and proved by consulting the laws of England and that (*B*) is an expression of an emotional reaction by the person who utters the statement and who alone can directly experience the feeling which the statement expresses. (*A*) is objective and (*B*) is subjective. But what are we to say of (*C*)? We cannot say that it is just like (*A*) because we cannot produce conclusive evidence in its favour or indeed any evidence at all that would be generally accepted. Now the way that we learn to recognize objective statements and distinguish them from subjective ones is precisely by learning which kinds of statement can be publicly checked in this way and which cannot. Since (*C*) falls into the latter class, must we not say that it is, after all, just like (*B*), a mere expression of personal emotion, however natural and common? And if we deny this and claim that it cannot be merely this, since sensible people do not argue to convince each other over matters of taste or private emotional responses, may we not be like the children arguing about whether marmalade is nice or nasty? The philosopher who holds a subjective view of moral judgments may well claim that he is just in the position of the sensible adult who sees the absurdity of this childish dispute.

I think it is clear that as long as we assume that moral judgments lie somewhere on a scale of objectivity, so to speak, between hard concrete statements of public fact at one end and private expressions of taste or emotion at the other, we shall never arrive at a proper conception of them. There can be no such scale; and statements cannot be more or less objective or indeed more or less subjective. A statement is objective if its truth is established or made probable by one kind of evidence and subjective if it is established by quite another kind. But a statement of value is not to be established either by the public inter-personal information of law courts and laboratories or by the private intimations of my own moods and feelings. If we try to prove that moral judgments are objective and inter-personal, by stressing their similarities to factual statements, the subjectivist will very properly stress the equally significant differences between them. And if we try to assimilate morals to matters of taste or to emotional responses, the objectivist will rightly remind us how very different they are in certain crucial ways. In particular, he will point out that moral judgments are not merely descriptions of my habitual or momentary states of mind. They are in some sense prescriptive or mandatory and not only for me but for everyone. The objectivist wants to claim that moral judgments can be proved—and this is manifestly false. The subjectivist wants to say that these things are matters of taste or at least of incommunicable personal experience and that such matters are proverbially beyond dispute. But this view is clearly an inadequate and indeed irrelevant description of what most of us suppose at least our own value judgments to express.

IV

So far we have confined our attention to the fact-stating uses of language and we have seen that they do not give us a satisfactory account of value statements. For whether we suppose that the facts stated are public or private, the account of value judgments that follows is patently inadequate. Let us therefore look at some of the other uses of language to see whether we may not get a more satisfactory view of value statements by taking account of these uses. Everyone would agree that although the communication of the observable facts of experience is a necessary function of language, it is not its only function or, indeed, its only important one. When we are engaged in most rational activities, it is natural enough to centre our attention on this informative use of language for it does not seem obvious how other uses could be relevant. This is not the place to take a survey of all the purposes that language serves. It will be sufficient here if we consider two of them.

Sometimes we use language to *express* or *evince* our feelings and attitudes and we sometimes do so in order to *influence* the feelings and attitudes of others. The first of these, which may be called the *expressive* function of language, must be sharply distinguished from its use in *describing* our private feelings or in *stating* that we have them. The expressive use of signs is much more primitive than the descriptive. A dog who snarls or wags his tail is showing or evincing his hostility or his pleasure, though lacking language, he cannot state that he feels these emotions or describe them to his audience. We may appreciate the distinction between the expressive and the informative uses by noticing that a man may easily use language so as to deny by one of these uses what he is affirming by the other. For example, he may shout in a temper: 'I'm perfectly calm, damn you!' or say: 'I have no prejudice against niggers or dagoes' evincing by his use of the emotively toned words 'nigger' and 'dago' the prejudice that he claims to repudiate. Thus though we may express our emotions and attitudes without any use of language as, for instance, by blushing, scowling or cheering, we very commonly do use language expressively. The expressive use is not incompatible with the informative, as is shown in the examples above and often, indeed, the two uses go so closely together so that it is a matter of some importance to be able to sort out in a given utterance the factual imformation conveyed from the expression of the speaker's attitude.

The second language use that was mentioned above is its use in influencing the actions and attitudes of other people, or, for that matter, of the speaker himself. In very simple cases, this will consist in giving orders. ('Shut the door!', 'Stand to attention!') But obviously we can use language to influence others in less crude ways. Polite requests, hints, indirect expressions of wishes and rhetoric of all kinds from the crudities of politicians and advertisers to the highest levels of literature may all be used for this end. Let us call all such uses of language *persuasive* uses, bearing in mind that this term covers a very wide and varied class of linguistic performances. It is clear that in practice there is a close connexion between the expressive and the persuasive functions of language. Human emotions and attitudes are infectious and whether they are expressed in words or in other ways may easily be communicated to an audience. This is indeed the main purpose of political speeches or of sermons. Thus people may be brought to share our

63

emotions and attitudes by the use of emotive language so that the expressive and the persuasive uses of words are intimately bound up together.

These facts of the natural history of language are familiar enough, but we need to see how they are connected with the problem of value judgments. Their relevance is shown by two theories on the nature of such judgments that have been put forward in recent years. We saw that both the subjectivist and the objectivist theories assume that a moral judgment states a fact and that they both fail precisely because they do assume this. But the theories of which I am now speaking claim that moral judgments are not statements of fact at all and that it makes no sense to ask of them whether they are true or false. The simplest of these theories points to the expressive uses of language and claims that moral statements like 'Stealing is wrong' or 'It is right to keep one's promises' are not genuine statements at all but mere *expressions* of moral approval or disapproval.

> The presence of an ethical symbol in a proposition adds nothing to its factual content. Thus if I say to someone, 'You acted wrongly in stealing that money', I am not stating anything more than if I had simply said, 'You stole that money.' In adding that this action is wrong I am not making any further statement about it. I am simply evincing my moral disapproval of it. It is as if I had said, 'You stole that money', in a peculiar tone of horror, or written it with the addition of some special exclamation marks. The tone, or the exclamation marks, adds nothing to the meaning of the sentence. It merely serves to show that the expression of it is attended by certain feelings in the speaker.[1]

This account of moral judgments, satirically named 'the Boo-Hurrah Theory', has been more successful in exciting hostility than in attracting serious criticism. Some critics have claimed to detect in it a cynical lack of moral seriousness. But moralizing

[1] A. J. Ayer: *Language, Truth and Logic* (Second Edition, 1946), p. 107.

of this kind cannot rank as a philosophical criticism of a theory; and in any case the appearance of cynicism is misleading as well as irrelevant. The reason why this simple and radical suggestion has been taken seriously by philosophers is not that it has ever seemed to tell the whole truth about the nature of moral judgments, but rather that it fills a very important logical gap ignored by the more traditional theories that we have already considered. We have seen that one of the puzzling features of moral statements is that disagreement about them so often persists after we have removed all disagreement about the observable facts of the situation in dispute. And for the reasons we have already considered, the so-called 'moral facts' of the situation, the rightness or wrongness of the action in question, can neither be inferred logically from the empirical facts nor constitute another class of 'nonnatural' facts alongside of them. It is therefore tempting to suppose that these elusive moral facts or qualities lie in something that is logically incapable of being verified or falsified by evidence. And we have just such a feature of the situation in an expression of attitude or moral emotion. It is logically incapable of being verified or falsified because, not being a statement, it is neither true nor false.

The exponents of this view claim that uttering a moral judgment like 'X is right' where X is a certain action or class of actions is akin to taking sides with or voting for X; and that, in so far as it can be regarded as a statement at all, it is more like an affirmation of the speaker's affiliations, loyalties or principles than a statement about the action. And to vote for or take sides with some action or policy is not to make or imply any statement that can be confirmed or refuted.

Yet on two counts the theory as it stands is inadequate. In the first place, we saw that one of the reasons that make us want to say that moral qualities are objective, public and independent of human thinking is that judgments about morals do claim to be more than a mere expression of a private attitude or preference. I do indeed express a preference when I say, for example, 'Cruelty to animals is wicked', but I claim in addition

65

that everyone else ought to share this preference. And this would be an absurd and impertinent claim to make about my private tastes and interests. The expressive theory of morals has therefore to be expanded or supplemented in some way to account for this necessary feature of moral language. Secondly, because moral judgments make a public claim in this way, they can be *supported by reasons*. We have somehow to show that as well as being expressive, moral judgments are (*a*) inter-personal and (*b*) capable of rational support. An attempt to develop the expressive theory to meet these defects has been worked out in some detail and the main point of the theory can be sketched in a summary and necessarily inadequate way as follows.[1] When I utter a moral judgment of the form 'X is right' where X is any action or class of actions of which I approve, my judgment has three functions. First, it expresses my own attitude to the action or even states that I have the attitude. That is, 'X is right' expresses or states my approval of X. Secondly the judgment has an *imperative* element. It directs my hearers to approve also. But it is clearly useless merely to command anyone to experience an emotion or assume an attitude, since even if my hearers are prepared to obey my commands, emotions and attitudes cannot be assumed at will. However the emotive or expressive component of the judgment works together with the imperative component to influence the audience by communicating to them some of my own attitude of approval. In this way, the first two components of the judgment working together have a persuasive effect which either would lack without the other.

Stated in this crude and simplified way, the amended theory seems to do no more than add an imperative element to the expressive account of moral judgments discussed above. But Stevenson shows further that if we take account also of the descriptive or informative force of moral words like 'good', 'bad', 'right' and 'wrong', it is possible to show how our *beliefs*

[1] The original version of this theory is due to Professor C. L. Stevenson and is argued by him very fully in his book *Ethics and Language* (New Haven, U.S.A., 1944).

about matters of fact are related to our *attitudes* about morals and how these beliefs and attitudes influence each other. In this way, a careful and detailed study of the complexities of actual moral discourse and of the relations between the informative, expressive and persuasive uses of language can throw new light on the central problem of moral philosophy, the problem of showing how our value judgments can be justified.

V

We can restate this problem of the justification of value judgments by asking: What sort of reasons are good reasons for a moral decision, or, more generally, what part does reason play in ethics? This is, of course, a traditional problem of moral philosophy and a most difficult one. It cannot be said that any philosopher has yet given a solution of it that is both convincing and complete. But the claim that moral judgments may best be interpreted as expressive or as persuasive discourse helps to remove the serious logical difficulties that were disregarded by those philosophers who insisted on looking on such judgments as plain factual statements, whether of an ordinary or a 'non-natural' kind. Moreover the work of Stevenson and his critics[1] has shown that the question is extremely complex and that no simple and dogmatic answer to it will suffice. I shall end this chapter by pointing to some difficulties that arise from attempts to answer the main question in order to emphasize that the question is still an open one. Even the most plausible account of moral judgments as persuasive expressions of attitudes is apt to seem unconvincing on one point at least. It has often been pointed out that though an expression of emotion or attitude by its very nature cannot be labelled 'true' or 'false', nevertheless attitudes are nearly always based upon beliefs about facts. And these beliefs *must* be either true or false. If, for example, I am afraid, it is because I believe that something threatens my safety. If I am angry, it is because I believe that someone has purposely harmed me or thwarted my interests. If I am loyal to a person or an institution, it is because

[1] See Bibliographical Note to Chapter 3.

I believe that the object of my loyalty has certain qualities (which I believe worthy of approval and support). Such beliefs may well be false but they must at least exist if we are not to regard the emotion or attitude in question as simply a neurotic symptom. There is thus a clear sense in which we can call on someone to justify his attitudes. We should be asking not indeed that he should show that his *attitude* was true but that he should show that it was well-grounded in being based on true beliefs about the world. And nothing in the theories we have been discussing tends to show that moral emotions and attitudes are any different from non-moral *in this respect*. Yet it is precisely here that theories of this kind seem to fail. For we do not justify the attitude expressed by a moral judgment merely by showing that the beliefs that account for the attitude are true. If this were so, we could always settle moral questions by determining the relevant facts; and we have already seen that such questions can usually *not* be decided in this way. The reason for this is important. It is that the facts that explain or account for a moral attitude are not necessarily regarded as *justifying* the attitude. Let us suppose, for example, that a South African advocate of racial discrimination defends his attitude by the claim that the economic stability of his country depends on the unequal treatment of black and white. This claim is probably true and his belief in its truth may well *account for* his moral attitude to racial inequality. But most people would object that this was quite irrelevant to the moral issue. Even though the belief was true and *caused* his attitude, it did not *justify* it.

Commonsense morality at least, though it may be in error on this point, wants to distinguish sharply between causal explanations of attitudes and moral justifications of them. Now Stevenson's theory does show how moral disagreements may be resolved by a combination of language uses. But to show how a dispute about morals may be brought to an end is not necessarily to show how a moral judgment may be validated. We saw above that it is necessary to distinguish the cause of a moral attitude from a justification of it. We now have to recognize a special case of this distinction, namely the difference between *persuading* someone to adopt a certain moral point of view and *justifying* that point of view. It seems paradoxical to claim that the process of justifying or validating moral judgments can ever be reduced to the interplay, however subtle and complex, of the informative, the expressive and the persuasive uses of language. For to claim this looks very like repeating in a disguised form the error, exposed by Hume, of trying to deduce value statements from statements of fact.

Let us consider the sort of reasoning by which we often try to justify our value judgments. In general, questions about morals arise at two levels. (1) We may ask ourselves: Is this particular action X wrong (or right)? And whether we answer 'Yes' or 'No', we shall normally be prepared to justify our answer by showing that the action in question falls under a general rule. We shall perhaps say 'All actions of type A are wrong' adding 'And action X is of type A'. (2) We are then faced with a second question of a more general kind: Why are all actions of type A wrong? And this question demands that the general rule itself should be justified. But we must notice that the type of justification called for at level 1 is totally different in character from that called for at level 2. The first question is a demand for a justification of a particular judgment and the other calls for the justification of a rule or standard. We answer questions of type 1 in the first place by citing the rule or standard which we consider relevant to the case in question. An opponent may then challenge us in one (or both) of two ways. He may say (a) that the case does not fall under the rule cited; or (b) he may refuse to accept our rule. Suppose, for example, that two people are arguing on the question: Were Brutus and his fellow conspirators wrong in assassinating Julius Caesar? X says 'No, because Caesar was a tyrant and tyrannicide is morally permissible.' Y may reply either (a) by denying that Caesar was a tyrant (and thus claiming that the case does not fall under the rule cited) or (b) he may refuse to admit that it is morally permitted to assassinate tyrants. An argument of type (a) is not nearly so intractable a dispute as one of type (*b*) for we have excellent precedents for this sort of reasoning. Legal arguments are very often of just this type and they are settled by a combination of adducing facts, comparing precedents and amending definitions in the ways that were referred to in the first section of this chapter. Often indeed the decision may contain a certain arbitrary element if the facts turn out to be a very borderline case of the rule to be applied. In the case quoted above, the definition of 'tyrant' is clearly nothing like precise enough to enable us always to know if a given case of assassination is a case of tyrannicide. Nevertheless, disputes about the application of rules to cases are in principle decidable by the same sort of arguments as are used in courts of law. But how are we to deal with questions of type 2? Clearly we cannot do so by adducing more general rules; for this can enable us only to postpone our difficulty and not to evade it. Even if we try to bring all our moral rules under one very general one, for example, 'Always act to maximize happiness' or 'Always do the will of God', we shall in the end be faced with the task of justifying this super-rule.

Let us look at a very crude and simple analogy to our problem in order to bring out some of its difficulties. If someone asks 'How much do you weigh?' you might say 'One hundred and fifty pounds' or, if the question came from a foreigner, 'Sixty-eight kilos'. Clearly it would not make sense to ask 'Which is your correct weight, one hundred and fifty pounds or sixty-eight kilos?' Each answer is correct by a different standard. One could sensibly ask which of the two was correct for a particular community, though one could *not* ask which of the two was the correct standard *in general*. But one could sensibly ask which of the two was the *better* way of measuring weights, pounds and ounces or kilos and grams. 'Better' here would mean, of course, 'more convenient and useful'. And questions of this kind can very well be argued by adducing facts in evidence, those facts for example that are cited by supporters of a decimal system of weights and measures.

How far can we apply this sort of analogy to clarify our problem about moral judgments? We often do decide the

The Justification of Value Judgments

moral status of a particular action by applying a rule of moral conduct just as we decide the length or weight of a physical thing by applying the approved scales or standards to it. But as we saw above, the real difficulty does not lie in our judgments about particular cases. We know, in general, how to apply our standards. The difficulties arise when we ask: How do you defend or justify that moral rule? Do we, for example, consider that in preferring 'Love your enemies' to 'An eye for an eye' as principles of social conduct, we are making the same sort of preference as we make in preferring the metric system to the English system of measurements? We can indeed defend 'Love your enemies' just as we can defend the metric system by pointing to the consequences of adopting it. We often do use this sort of defence. But we feel nevertheless that to *persuade* our opponent to adopt a moral principle by such methods is not necessarily to convince him that it is *the right principle.* Honesty, for instance, may in fact be the best policy but its happy consequences alone do not show it to be a virtue. We want to insist that it would still be right even if it were not politic.

The doubts that we tend to feel about such empirical justifications of moral principles may be mere illusions. They may turn out to be no more than the residual effects of the old-fashioned objectivist theories of morals which provided the uncriticized background of most of our early training. But it would be dogmatic to insist that they *must* be no more than this. Recent work in ethics has shown quite conclusively why talk about 'objective moral standards' or 'the natural law' or 'the will of God' can solve no problems in morals and indeed that it diverts our attention from important issues. But the constructive parts of recent moral theories have not been so obvious or so effective as the critical parts. We still do not know all it means to say that a certain moral principle is 'right' or 'valid' or 'justifiable', though we know fairly well what this does not and cannot mean. For this reason, the problem of how to justify our value judgments is still an unsolved problem of philosophy. To realize this will save us from dogmatism and at the same time encourage us to go on looking for the answer.

4

THEORIES AND EXPLANATIONS

I

PHILOSOPHERS have traditionally been concerned, among other things, with questions about human knowledge. What are the objects of our knowing and believing? What are the various sources of our knowledge? For example, does all our knowledge come from sensation? Or are there other sources—memory, reason, introspection, intuition and so on? Are there any reliable differences between *knowing* something to be the case and merely *believing* it to be so? And if so, what are these differences? Are there basically different kinds of knowledge? If so, what are the different sorts of evidence appropriate to each of these kinds? We might believe, for example, (*a*) that every angle drawn in a semicircle contains ninety degrees and (*b*) that the moon is about 240,000 miles distant from the earth. But whereas evidence derived from observation and measurement would be appropriate to establish the truth of (*b*) it would not be sufficient or even appropriate to prove the truth of (*a*).[1] And arising from this, if there are different kinds of evidence appropriate to different kinds of statement, are there also different kinds of truth? And if there are, what are these different kinds and how are they to be identified and described?

All these questions and many other of the same kind have

[1] For this we need a general deductive proof of the sort familiar in school geometry.

been discussed by philosophers under the general label 'epistemology' or 'theory of knowledge'. In particular, since the rise and development of the sciences, philosophers have interested themselves especially in the reliable and systematic bodies of knowledge elaborated in the various sciences and have asked such questions as the following: What are the characteristic features of scientific explanation? What is a theory? How are we to distinguish good theories from bad ones?

They have asked these questions and many others like them because science is a spectacularly successful way of knowing and so falls into one of the philosophers' general fields of interest. Some of them have supposed indeed that the sort of knowledge that science gives us is to be regarded as a standard or ideal by reference to which other less perfect kinds of knowledge may be compared and criticized. However this may be, the activities of scientists are of great value and interest to philosophers who are concerned with problems of human knowledge. It is commonly said that if we are to be justified in claiming that a certain person X *knows* a certain proposition p, three conditions must be satisfied. (i) p must be true. (ii) X must *believe* that p is true. (iii) X must have *evidence that justifies his belief* that p is true. It is easy enough to provide examples from our everyday beliefs of (i) and (ii). But it is not nearly so easy to give examples from our everyday beliefs that satisfy the third condition. Sometimes, in such cases, we should find it very difficult to assemble the evidence for our beliefs. And even where we can collect the evidence and put it into some sort of order, we should probably find it very difficult to show that the evidence *justified* the belief in question.

But we can easily collect from the elementary stages of the natural sciences true propositions that are believed by all competent scientists and for which evidence can be presented in a form that can be understood by persons unskilled in the appropriate sciences. Moreover the systematic way in which the science is presented displays the logical relations between the propositions. Thus there certainly is a sense in which a developed science is *a* paradigm of human knowledge (though

F   73

to admit this is not to commit ourselves to the debatable statement that it is the *only* paradigm).

Philosophers consider scientific theories from the outside as it were, with reference to the rules and standards that govern the formation and testing of such theories. This is not to say, of course, that it is in any sense their task to criticize the findings of the scientists or to guide their work. Science is a self-correcting procedure and needs no advice or criticism of this kind from outside. It is rather that the philosopher uses the theoretical achievements of the scientist to widen, illustrate and make precise his own conceptions of knowledge. His work does however enable him to give some help to those less developed or even embryonic sciences whose methods and standards are imperfectly worked out. The physicist, chemist or astronomer is rarely interested in the progress or methods of less developed sciences like psychology or sociology. And often he has not even the time or interest to reflect on his own methods and standards of explanation as long as they work satisfactorily. It is in this sort of necessary liaison work between the more developed and the less developed sciences that the philosopher's post-mortems on the achievements of natural science can be very valuable. Provided that he has some very necessary familiarity with the sciences in question, he can collate and compare the various methods and standards of explanation used in the various sciences, natural and social. And this natural history of method can be useful, as we shall see, in testing the value of theories in a field like education where the sciences applied are necessarily of a primitive and rudimentary kind. In such cases, theories do not confirm or refute themselves, as they do in a well-developed science.

II

I want now to consider the word 'theory' which takes such a prominent place in expositions of scientific achievement. My main purpose in doing so will be eventually to make clear, as far as this is possible, what job an *educational* theory is supposed to do. But since education is not (and is not claimed to be) an

74

exact science and does not even rely to any large extent upon the findings of such sciences, the word 'theory' is used in educational contexts in a derivative and weakened sense. What this sense (or senses) are, we can most easily see by considering first the uses of the word 'theory' in the contexts of the natural sciences where it occurs at its strongest and clearest.

In ordinary speech, the word is used both ambiguously and vaguely. That is to say, it has several (though related) meanings and no one of these is perfectly clear cut. These different senses are not all equally relevant for our purposes but because the fallacy of 'one word—one meaning' is still so widespread, it will be useful to distinguish the main senses of the word. (1) Sometimes the word is used, as in philosophy, to mean no more than 'a body of related problems'. It is in this sense that philosophers talk of 'the theory of knowledge' or 'the theory of value'. (2) It may also be used to refer to a very highly organized and unified conceptual framework with little or no relation to any practical activity. For example, mathematicians talk of 'the theory of numbers' or of 'group theory'. (3) When in ordinary speech we contrast theory with practice we refer to a set or system of rules or a collection of precepts which guide or control actions of various kinds. In some fields of action, such a theoretical background is more useful and necessary than in others. Obviously, a physician or an electrical engineer has more need of theory in this sense of the word than a plumber or a carpenter. Yet there are handbooks on plumbing or carpentry that can be said to contain the 'theory' of these crafts. Such theories would differ from those underlying the practice of medicine or of plant breeding or violin playing chiefly in being (*a*) less complex and (*b*) less unified and systematic. They would probably amount to little more than a set of rules of thumb. In this sense of the word, we might properly contrast the theory of education with its practice. Educational theory would then consist of those parts of psychology concerned with perception, learning, concept formation, motivation and so on which directly concern the work of the teacher. In this vague sense of the word, then, 'theory' means a general conceptual background to some field of practical activity. And such a conceptual background is usually in some degree unified and systematic so that parts of the theory are logically related to other parts. This degree of system will naturally be highest in a highly developed science like physics. (4) There is however a more technical sense of the word 'theory' which it is useful to consider here because it is a sense that gives us standards by which we can assess the value and use of any claimant to the title of 'theory'. In particular, this sense of the word will enable us to judge the value of the various (and often conflicting) theories that are put forward by writers on education. The model or paradigm of theories in this, the most important, sense of the word is to be found in natural science and particularly in the more developed sciences like physics or astronomy. Even in these restricted fields, the word 'theory' has no one perfectly definite meaning. But it is most often used to refer (*a*) to a hypothesis that has been verified by observation and, more commonly, (*b*) to a logically interconnected set of such confirmed hypotheses.

III

'Hypothesis' is a Greek work for 'supposition' or, in plain English, 'guess'. But not every kind of guess is a hypothesis. The word is used to refer to those rational conjectures that are found to be of use in solving problems that arise in the course of scientific enquiry. It is found in practice that these conjectures must satisfy certain conditions if they are to serve their purpose. Consider a simple example from a nontechnical context. Suppose that I am driving my car and I notice that the engine is losing power. Remembering my previous experience of this sort of thing, I may say to myself: 'Perhaps the sparking plugs need cleaning.' This expresses a hypothesis, viz. that dirt on the plugs is the cause of the loss of power in the engine. I can then test this hypothesis by taking the plugs from the engine and examining them. If I find them covered in carbon or oil, I can clean and replace them and then test the engine again. If it recovers its normal performance,

I am justified in saying: '*Probably* the dirt on the plugs was the cause of the loss of power.' If on the other hand the car pulls no more strongly than it did before, I can say: 'The dirt on the plugs was not the cause or, at least, not the *only* cause of the loss of power.' Similarly if on removing the plugs I find them perfectly clean, I conclude that whatever caused the loss of power, it was *not* dirt on the plugs.

This sort of procedure is a familiar way of accounting for unusual incidents that arise in the course of our everyday experience. It is important to notice its essential features. (1) The hypothesis is not an unmotivated, undirected or random guess. It is designed to lead to an answer to a particular question. In this case, the question is: What causes the car to lose power? (2) The hypothesis is always such that, if true, it will have *observable consequences*. (Conversely, if false, the anticipated consequences will *not* be observed.) If would, for example, be a genuine rival hypothesis in the instance I have given if it was suggested that there was a fault in the electrical wiring of the engine. For this suggestion could also be confirmed or refuted by observation. But it would *not* be a genuine alternative hypothesis if someone, perhaps an African tribesman, were to suggest that the engine was possessed by an evil spirit. For no conceivable observations would enable us to confirm or refute this suggestion.[1] (3) For the hypothesis to be a valid one, the anticipated consequences must actually occur. But it should

[1] It is important to be clear why this is so. Suppose that car engines were to stop every time a certain spell was uttered over them and were to start again whenever another spell was uttered. If this happened regularly and if we could disprove any other hypothesis about the cause of the cars' behaviour, we might be forced in the end to accept a general law of the kind: Spell A stops car engines and spell B starts them. For we could *observe* the sequence: engine running, utterance of spell A, engine stopping, utterance of spell B, engine starting.

Thus hypotheses about magical causes and effects are not *in principle* beyond proof, though we do not seem ever to meet with the evidence that would establish them. But the state of affairs imagined above would not, by itself, support the hypothesis that the engine was possessed by an evil spirit. (Why not?)

be noted that the fact that the consequences deduced from the hypothesis (in the case cited, the presence of dirt on the sparking plugs) *are* actually observed does not *conclusively* establish that the hypothesis is correct. It merely renders it more or less probable, depending upon the nature of the hypothesis and the circumstances in which the confirming observation is made. The argument: 'If hypothesis H is true, then a certain fact F will be observed; and F is observed: therefore H is true', is formally invalid. On the other hand, if the observed facts do *not* confirm the prediction implicit in the hypothesis, then the hypothesis is *conclusively* refuted (at least in the precise form in which it is put). For the argument: 'If hypothesis H is true, then a certain fact F will be observed; and F is *not* observed: therefore H is *not* true' is a valid one.

This method of accounting for unusual facts is a very characteristic pattern of scientific, as well as of everyday, thinking. It contains three steps: (1) the proposal of a hypothesis to account for an unexpected or anomalous fact; (2) the deduction from this hypothesis that certain other facts are observable; (3) the checking of this deduction by observation. This pattern of thinking is often called 'the hypothetical-deductive method'. The example taken above from our everyday experience may suggest by its very simplicity that scientific thinking is no more than commonsense ways of thinking employed about rather specialized and restricted topics. There is no doubt a sense in which this is true, and the well-known description of science as 'organized common sense' is intended to epitomize this suggestion. Nevertheless the problems that confront scientific workers in the laboratory or in the field are very different in important respects from the practical puzzles of everyday living. The differences are of three main kinds. (1) The questions that have to be answered are such as would occur only to observers familiar with the established theoretical background of the science in question. (2) The observations that give rise to the hypothesis, as well as those carried out to confirm it, usually require specially trained observers and often call for the use of elaborate and delicate instruments. (3) The

deductions made from the hypothesis may present great difficulties, both theoretical and practical, for example, mathematical calculations of great technical difficulty or of considerable length and complexity. An example taken from the
history of science will show both the characteristic differences
and the essential similarities between the commonsense use
of the hypothetical deductive method and its use in science.

In the year 1781, the planet Uranus was discovered by Sir
William Herschel. As soon as its discovery was announced,
astronomers began to collect observations in order to compute
its orbit and they were soon able to predict the path of the
new planet. But although the behaviour of Uranus at first
conformed to the predictions of the astronomers, it began after
a few years to diverge slightly from them. By the year 1840,
the discrepancies between the observed path of Uranus and its
predicted path were large enough to show that the behaviour
of the planet could not be accounted for by the gravitational
forces that were then known to act upon it, that is to say, the
gravitational pulls due to the sun and to those planets known
at that time. But it is important to notice that although the
discrepancy between observation and prediction was sufficiently large by 1840 to need an explanation, it was still far too
small to be observed by the naked eye. (It amounted at that date
to about ninety seconds of arc or one part in thirty six hundred
of a right angle.)

Various hypotheses were proposed to account for this
divergence between theory and observation. One suggestion
among several was that a very distant and hitherto unobserved
planet existed whose gravitational attraction for Uranus caused
the perturbations of its orbit from the expected course. Now
it is a difficult computation for an astronomer to work out the
perturbations of a planetary orbit caused by another planet of
known weight, size and position. But to perform the inverse
calculation and deduce from the observed irregularities of one
planet's orbit the size and position of another yet unobserved
planet which causes them is a very much more formidable task.
And to do this over a hundred years ago without the assistance

of modern calculating machines was a mathematical feat of the highest distinction. Yet two astronomers, J. C. Adams in Cambridge and Leverrier in France, carried out this calculation independently of each other and predicted the position in the sky where the new planet might be seen with a telescope. It remained to carry out the third step of the hypothetical deductive scheme and confirm by observation the existence of the new planet in its predicted place. Even this was not a straightforward and easy task. It needed a good telescope, a trained observer and an accurate star map. The search was not systematically undertaken until nearly a year after Adams had completed his calculations. In September 1846 Galle in Berlin, acting on a suggestion from Leverrier, made the predicted observation, and a new planet, later to be called Neptune, was discovered.

It is easy to see that the main steps in this classical scientific achievement correspond exactly to those in the trivial incident of the motor car cited above. We have in each case (*a*) an observed divergence from our expectations; (*b*) a hypothesis proposed to account for this unusual event; (*c*) deduction from the hypothesis of an *observable* consequence; (*d*) the making of an observation to check the deduction. The difference between the two cases lies (i) in the immense complexity and technical difficulty of making both the necessary deductions and the necessary observations in the case of the scientific hypothesis; (ii) in the fact that the scientific hypothesis arises in a context of well-established scientific theory (in this case, the Newtonian theory of gravitation). Except to a skilled astronomer, the perturbations of the orbit of Uranus would not have been noticeable nor, if they had been noticed, would they have had any significance. They derive their significance from the fact that they are at variance with what is to be expected *in the light of what has already been established as theory*.

The hypothesis of the existence of Neptune and the verification of that hypothesis gives a particularly clear example of the working of the hypothetical deductive method in science.

Yet the hypothesis itself is not perhaps a characteristic scientific hypothesis in that, in this example, *one particular fact* is hypothesized and subsequently verified. We certainly would not ordinarily refer to the established fact of the existence of Neptune as a *theory*.[1] But many hypotheses in science, and those the most important ones, suggest not the existence of particular facts but the operation of general laws. For example, one of Kepler's laws about planetary motion states that *all* planets travel in elliptical orbits; Boyle's law states that for *all* gases, volume and pressure are inversely proportional when the temperature is kept constant; and so on. And the more common use of the word 'theory' applies it to a logically interconnected set of such laws. The theory of planetary motion, for example, would comprise Kepler's laws about the motion of planets, which are themselves instances of more general laws of motion applying to any material bodies under any conditions. These wider laws make up the theory of classical mechanics. The commonest use of the word 'theory', then, applies it to a body of interconnected laws where the word 'law' is being used in its standard scientific sense to refer to an observable uniformity of nature. And the usual method of establishing such laws is by the hypothetical deductive method described above. We have now to ask: What is the function of a scientific theory?

IV

There seems to be fairly general agreement among the scientists and philosophers who write about scientific method that theories fulfil three functions (1) description, (2) prediction, and (3) explanation. However, they do not all agree on which of these three uses of a theory is the most basic. Some claim for example that science is essentially descriptive,

[1] We might indeed refer to the existence of the electron or of the unconscious as a theory but we would then be hypothesizing not particular facts but a structure *common* to all atoms or to all human minds. Or perhaps it might be said that in these cases we are hypothesizing particular facts only in so far as they are illustrative of the supposed common structure.

others that it is predictive or that it is explanatory. But whether or not such disputes are useful, it is easy to see that all three functions are interconnected. It is indeed not difficult to understand the sense in which science can properly be claimed both to be descriptive and to be predictive. Boyle's law, cited above, does describe the behaviour of gases under varying conditions of pressure with constant temperature. It does also enable us to predict the way in which volumes of gas, hitherto unobserved, will behave under such conditions of temperature and pressure. Any well established scientific law can be regarded both as a summary of past experience and as a guarantee of future experience. But it is much less simple to give an account of the sense in which scientific laws (and therefore, scientific theories) are explanatory. The nature of explanation is not so obvious as the nature of description and prediction.

Facts and events are said to demand explanation when, for one reason or another, they puzzle us. But there are a number of ways of removing puzzlement in the face of the unfamiliar and yet other ways of removing the more profound and important kind of puzzlement that we sometimes feel in the face of familiar happenings. Some of these ways are genuine and adequate modes of explanation and others are not. It is important that we should have some ways of distinguishing genuine from bogus explanations. There is a well-known passage in Professor Basil Willey's book *The Seventeenth Century Background* that will help to introduce some of the important questions connected with explanation.

The clarity of an explanation seems to depend on the degree of satisfaction that it affords. An explanation 'explains' best when it meets some need of our nature, some deep seated demand for assurance. 'Explanation' may perhaps be roughly defined as a restatement of something—event, theory, doctrine, etc.—in terms of the current interests and assumptions. . . . All depends upon our presuppositions, which in turn depend upon our training whereby we have come to regard (or to feel) one set of terms as ultimate, the other not. . . . One cannot therefore define 'explanation' absolutely; one can only say that it is a statement that satisfies the demand of a particular time or place.

Clearly, Professor Willey is writing here as a historian of ideas and not as a philosopher.

However, we can learn something from his errors, especially as they are characteristic of popular thinking on this point. He implies that it is a necessary condition of an explanation that it should bring what has to be explained into harmony with our beliefs or 'presuppositions'. He also implies that this is a sufficient mark of an explanation. Further the 'clarity' of an explanation depends upon its effect on us—'on the degree of satisfaction that it affords'. The criterion of an explanation on his view is a purely psychological one. It is a good one if it has certain effects on the people to whom it is directed. But there is no suggestion that there is any difference between good and bad explanations except in terms of the effects on the audience. He does insist, it is true, that explanations get their effects by harmonizing with the 'presuppositions' of those to whom they are addressed but he seems to think it quite irrelevant whether such presuppositions are true or false. Thus, for example, an explanation of a plague epidemic in terms of witchcraft would harmonize with the presuppositions of an African tribe and would be a good one if addressed to such an audience. An explanation in terms of bacterial infection carried by fleas would, to the same audience, be a bad one.

It is clear that such an account of explanation is not only false but also mischievous. By failing to distinguish true explanations from false ones, it makes it impossible for anyone who takes the account seriously to make any progress at all in explaining the world. It is not perhaps surprising to find that Professor Willey's aim in expounding this account is to depreciate the change of world outlook effected by the work of Galileo and the seventeenth-century scientists and to claim that the scholastic world view which they refuted was an equally good explanation of the facts. To take the example he offers, whether we prefer Galileo's explanation of the spots on the moon in terms of extinct volcanoes or the contemporary theologians' explanation in terms of the will of God is merely a matter of whether we prefer Galileo's presuppositions to those of his opponents. Relative to their respective presuppositions, these two explanations are equally good ones.

But there is, in this account, one true assumption that is worth extracting as a basis for a more reliable analysis of the nature of explanation. The assumption is that since one of the purposes of explanation is to remove puzzlement, the explanation must relate the proposition that is found puzzling to the rest of what we know. There are, as we shall see, various ways in which what has to be explained, the *explicandum*, as it is often called, may be related to our present knowledge. However, if the explanation is to be a true one, it is essential that the *explicandum* should be thus related to what we *know* and not to what we mistakenly *believe*. It follows from this that to a person whose relevant beliefs are faulty, *no explanation can be given*. We could not explain the causes of a plague epidemic to people who believed that all diseases were caused by witchcraft and who had never heard of bacterial or virus infection. In such cases, the process of explanation has to start with re-education. This sort of case occurs more frequently than might be supposed. The scepticism of the man in the street about scientific explanations is often due not to hardheaded commonsense or a naturally critical turn of mind or to any other intellectual virtue; it is often due merely to ignorance of the relevant theoretical and factual background. And ignorance of this kind will disqualify anyone from appreciating the logical force of an explanation.

One of the main tasks of any explanation then is to link up the *explicandum* with what we already know and understand. This 'linking up' may be done, as we shall see, in several different ways. But however it is done, the explanation will fail unless it succeeds in making more intelligible what was previously found to be, in one way or another, difficult to understand. A very common example of this occurs when we explain unusual conduct in terms of the *purposes* of the person whose behaviour puzzles us. If we were to see a man in conventional city dress dive into the river from Westminster Bridge, we should naturally ask for an explanation of his behaviour. And we should take as a satisfactory explanation that he was trying to rescue a would-be suicide or to win a bet or to escape from the police or some such story. Explanations of this kind are acceptable because they reduce what is apparently exceptional to an instance of a more familiar type. We are all acquainted in our own experience with purposive action. Indeed, we are so well acquainted with it that we are apt to invoke explanations in terms of purpose where they are quite inappropriate. In science, their use is very small indeed.

It is probably unwise to try to classify the explanations that are found to be successful in science under clear-cut labels. Nevertheless, there do seem to be four general ways in which an explanation of this sort can be effected.

1 The first type occurs where we explain a single anomalous fact (or a small group of such facts) by showing that it is after all not exceptional but is an instance of a general law. Sometimes the law may be a well known one and sometimes it may be quite new. An example of the first kind would be an explanation of the fact that a balloon filled with hydrogen rises in air instead of falling. To an intelligent child to whom this phenomenon was a novelty, one might say: 'It is just like a piece of wood floating on water. *Any* body immersed in *any* fluid is subjected to an upthrust equal to the weight of the fluid it displaces. This means that materials lighter than water float in water and materials lighter than air float in air and so on.' Or to take an example of the second kind (where the law is not well known) we might try to explain a case of serious misbehaviour in a school child by pointing out that the child lived in a slum and that bad housing conditions were known to be associated in a high proportion of cases with delinquency in children. We find this sort of procedure enlightening, though to a more limited degree than the first, just because we know that, by and large,

the events in nature occur in regular patterns. If therefore an apparently exceptional event can be shown to be an instance of an established regularity we find this reassuring, even if the regularity was one previously unknown to us. But this is clearly a fairly primitive level of explanation and it is more easily exemplified from the less developed sciences. For this sort of thing does not usually satisfy us for long. We next want to ask for an explanation of the regularity that is invoked to explain the fact. In the advanced sciences, it is often possible to satisfy this request.

2 This usually involves explaining a law of nature as an instance of a still more general law. For example, Kepler's laws of planetary motion can be said to be *explained* when they are shown to follow from Newton's mechanics as a special case of the Newtonian theory. Similarly, the Newtonian theory was itself explained in this way by the theory of relativity. Another well known instance of this sort of explanation by generalization occurred when Clerk Maxwell showed, in the middle of the last century, that the equations that he had devised to satisfy the phenomena of electromagnetism also satisfied the phenomena of light. He unified in this way two previously separate branches of science into one by devising a wider theory of which two previously known theories could be shown to be special cases. Advanced sciences like chemistry and physics give us frequent cases of explanation of this sort. Other instances will readily occur to students of these sciences.

A theory that can in this way generalize a more restricted theory or unify two or more less general theories is usually of necessity both simpler and more abstract than the theories that it explains. It is however important that a unifying theory should not be so general that it loses its connexion with observable fact. One very general 'theory' which could purport to explain *all* natural phenomena would be that every change observed in the universe was due to the direct agency of God. Such a suggestion was, indeed, made in the seventeenth century by the so-called 'occasionalists', philosophers influenced by the doctrines of Descartes. But a theory of this kind by trying to explain everything ends by explaining nothing at all. For it is compatible with any possible observation that we might care to make. In other words, since it cannot be refuted by any possible observation, it cannot be confirmed by one either; which is to say that experience is irrelevant to its truth or falsity and that accordingly it is not a genuine scientific theory at all. But not all such over-general 'theories' are so patently empty as this one. Some of them can masquerade in more convincing guises especially in those social sciences relevant to education where the rules of method are not always so closely looked to as they must be in the sciences of nature.

In the two types of explanation looked at so far, the logical feature common to them both will have been obvious. Whether we explain a single fact or set of similar facts by adducing a law of nature of which the facts are instances or whether we explain a law or theory by showing that it is an instance or special case of a more general theory, we are in each case finding a premiss from which the *explicandum* can be deduced as a conclusion. We explain a fact, law or theory by showing that it *follows from* a more general law or theory, whether or not such a more general law or theory is better known to us or not. The explanation may be psychologically more convincing if the *explicandum* can be shown to be a disguised instance of something quite familiar to us. But it is not therefore logically more cogent. The necessary conditions for the truth of any conclusion are: (1) the argument leading to the conclusion must be logically valid; (2) the premisses from which the conclusion is drawn must be true. If we are familiar with the premisses, the explanation will consist merely in putting the *explicandum* in a new light and thereby showing that it does in fact follow from what we already know. But provided that the premisses are true, it is logically irrelevant whether we happen to be familiar with them or not.

This point is not perhaps a very obvious one and a neglect of it accounts for the views of Professor Willey which we discussed above. Explanation is one kind of reasoning. Now the effectiveness of any sort of reasoning depends on two different kinds of conditions. The truth of the premises from which we reason and the validity of the logical rules in accordance with which we argue are matters independent of us. But since we undertake reasoning to find out what is true, our reasoning will be pointless unless we can *know* that the premises from which we start are true also. Thus the second kind of condition on which the effectiveness of reasoning depends is something which is not independent of us, namely, what we believe. Explanations cannot be effective in giving us understanding instead of puzzlement unless they relate the *explicanda* to what we already believe. But equally they cannot do their work of giving understanding unless what we believe is true and *demonstrably* true, that is, unless what we believe is also what we know.

This then is the main logical pattern underlying explanation. But I said above that there were four general ways in which explanations could be given and so far I have described only two of them. The two remaining patterns of explanation are not so logically basic as the two I described above but they may be looked on as useful ancillaries to them.

3 We are sometimes said to explain a set of facts that we find puzzling when we propose or construct a *model* to elucidate the way in which they work. The history of the physical sciences offers many examples of this sort of explanation and in recent years models have become important explanatory devices in the biological and even in the social sciences. The development of physics in the seventeenth century was helped by picture-thinking of this kind when the rival theories of light, the wave theory and the corpuscular theory were first propounded. Men understood in rough outline the way in which waves were propagated through water and also the way in which material particles like bullets could be propagated through space. And since it was found at first that the behaviour of light could be interpreted *as if* light behaved in either of these two familiar ways, both the wave model and the particle model of the propagation of light were used as explanations of optical phenomena. This is clearly an example

of something we have met already, that is to say, the explanation of the unfamiliar in terms of the familiar. It must be noticed however that this kind of explanation is only an aid to the development of theories and not the goal of science. Both the wave model and the particle model of light were of great importance in the development of physics in suggesting further hypotheses about the laws of optics and so leading to new discoveries and the consequent revision of previous theories. For example, Foucault argued in 1850 that if light really behaved as the wave model indicated, it would travel faster in air than in water. This suggested an experiment to test the relative velocities of light in air and in water which showed that light did in fact travel more slowly in the denser medium. Neither model has proved to be adequate by itself to explain all the optical phenomena observed during the present century. But they served their purpose for a long time in providing fresh and fruitful ways of thinking about puzzling events. These ways of thinking enabled scientists to assimilate the novelty of the events with which they had to deal and so explain them better in more comprehensive theories.

When a science reaches a very high level of development, as chemistry and physics have done, crude models drawn from our everyday experience cease to be of much value or interest. The resemblance in structure or working between the model and the facts to be explained tends to break down and the models lose their power of proposing new lines of experiment. The functions of the older mechanical or commonsense pictures are taken over at this level by mathematical formulae whose structural properties preserve in a more subtle and useful form the virtues of the picture type of model. But at lower levels of scientific thinking, explanatory models are a very useful method of developing old and less adequate theories into new and more adequate ones. And mechanical models of this sort have recently proved useful in such unlikely fields as psychology and economics. Electrical and electronic machines have recently been devised which can imitate a number of types of behaviour hitherto thought to be peculiar to living creatures. For example, purposive action, memory and primitive forms of learning have been closely paralleled by machines designed by Dr. R. W. Ashby and Dr. Grey Walter. And the remarkable advances in recent years in the design and construction of calculating machines have led to speculations about the possible correspondence in structure and capacities between such machines and the human brain.[1] The use of such models is to suggest *possible* ways in which the nervous systems of animals and men may be built and *possible* ways in which they may work, suggestions that may perhaps be checked by experiment. It is important however to remember that, of themselves, they tell us nothing about the laws governing human and animal behaviour. They merely suggest possible lines on which our knowledge of these laws could be improved. In economics, models are usually of the mathematical kind familiar to physicists but an ingenious hydraulic model—the Newlyn-Phillips machine—has been constructed to illustrate in a visual form the relations between the production, consumption, stocks and price of a commodity and the ways in which these factors interact. Thus models in science act like metaphors in language; they enlighten us by suggesting arguments by analogy from known resemblances to resemblances so far unnoticed. They may also act as aids to the type of explanation discussed below. But by themselves, they are no more than a useful stimulus to the process of explanation.

4   The last kind of explanation that I shall mention here has a more independent status than explanation by models. We explain two facts in this way when we *fill the gap* between them. The gap may be a gap in space when the two events happen in different places or a gap in time when they happen at different times. And, commonly, the gap is both spatial and temporal. Suppose a child asks you to explain how pressing the bell push at the front door causes a bell to ring inside the house. You would explain this by showing him the successive stages in the process; how pressing the bell push closes an electric

[1] A good popular account of this work is given in Dr. W. Sluckin's *Minds and Machines* (Penguin Books, 1954).

circuit and allows a current to run down the wire, how the current activates a magnet which then attracts the bell clapper thus breaking the circuit—and so on. This would not indeed be a final explanation, for you might have to explain to a persistent questioner how currents flow and how magnets can be actuated by currents and so on. And this would call for a different sort of explanation in terms of the laws of electromagnetism. Nevertheless, as a first step in explanation, showing 'how the wheels go round' is very helpful. Moreover, there are some sciences in which explanation at this level is basic and of the first importance. The so-called genetic or developmental sciences which include large parts of biology and psychology and economics and almost the whole of studies like history and anthropology depend for the explanations which they can give us on gap-filling stories of this kind.[1] To give an account of the working of a television set or the process of digestion or the origins of a neurosis or the causes of the Industrial Revolution or the influence of witchcraft in an African society or in a hundred and one other explanations of this familiar sort, we should have to start with an account of the gap-filling kind. And with many such cases we could go no further than this type of explanation. So it is important to notice that though this kind of explanation is, in an advanced science like physics, only a first step towards elucidating the facts and is often not required or even appropriate there, in the social sciences for which educational theory is a focus, it is of the first importance because we often have at present no more satisfactory pattern of explanation. This does not mean, of course, that we should therefore give up hope of finding one.

[1] There is more than one kind of genetic or 'gap-filling' explanation. But we can ignore these differences here.

5

WHAT IS AN EDUCATIONAL THEORY?

I

IN the previous chapter we discussed the different ways in which the word 'theory' is commonly used. We saw that in the strictest sense of the word, a theory is an established hypothesis or, more usually, a logically connected set of such hypotheses whose main function is to explain their subject matter. The object of this discussion was to find out what can be said about theories in education. For the word 'theory' is apt to be used there very freely but more loosely than in most other contexts. It will therefore be worthwhile finding out, if we can, both the different senses in which the term occurs there and also the extent to which it is used in its primary sense of an explanatory conceptual framework based on experience and when it is used only in some derivative and weakened sense. Because of the success of scientific modes of explanation, the word 'theory' has come to be a prestige word. Like most such words, it is used more often for its prestige value than for its strict descriptive sense. An examination of this kind will tell us when we are to take the word 'theory' seriously in an educational context and when we need not do so.

Most people would agree that education is not itself a science. It is rather a set of practical activities connected by a common aim. But such activities often have their theoretical justification in some scientific theory. Indeed, the more reliable and efficient a system of education becomes, the more firmly will its techniques and aims be grounded in scientific findings. In this respect, the practice of education may be compared with the practice of medicine or of engineering. Medicine again is not itself a science. It aims not at the increase of knowledge but at a practical result, the prevention and cure of disease. However, in order that doctors can carry out this task effectively, they have to make use of the relevant scientific discoveries in their practical techniques; and they have themselves to know a certain amount of the sciences that bear upon their work. In particular, they must know a good deal of anatomy and physiology, the sciences of the structure of the body and of its working. Again, if we look not at the physicians and surgeons themselves but at the medical research workers who develop the tools of the doctors' trade, we find that many of them are pure scientists and perhaps not even medically qualified. The growing points of medical knowledge lie largely in pure science, in physics, chemistry and physiology rather than in the day to day activities of the consulting room and the operating theatre.

The same is true of the relation between the practical techniques of the engineer and the theoretical discoveries of the scientist and the mathematician. If no more mathematics and physics was known today than was known three hundred years ago, we should be without practically all the mechanical advances that have marked off the nineteenth and twentieth centuries from the rest of history. There were of course doctors, surgeons and engineers in the ancient and medieval worlds. They had to work without the scientific equipment of their present-day counterparts and, as a result, the scope of their work and its efficacy was immeasurably less than that of modern doctors and engineers. Their skill and knowledge was based on what they and their predecessors could find out by trial and error in the course of their practice. This traditional skill and knowledge was rarely based on any sort of experimentally verified findings and in the case of medicine contained as a result a good deal of superstition and nonsense.

(Doctors and educators, unlike engineers, are not restrained by the nature of their failures from allowing their practice to outstrip its theoretical basis.)

How far can we use this analogy between education and other practical arts with a scientific basis? It might be tempting to suppose that since the sciences on which education rests are not in the advanced state of chemistry, physics and mathematics, great advances in educational theory and practice may be expected when the sciences of psychology and sociology attain maturity. Perhaps twentieth-century education is in the primitive condition of the engineering and medicine of the seventeenth and eighteenth centuries. We have made some advances in the relevant social sciences but so far, the advances have been modest ones and even so, they have not been properly applied in the service of education. More perfect knowledge and more systematic application of theory to practice may perhaps be expected to bring about an educational revolution. Some people would no doubt be willing to support this point of view but I think that there are good reasons for supposing that it is far too optimistic about the future and, moreover, far too pessimistic about the present.

What then is wrong with the proposed analogy? In one sense, the comparison is a fair one. Education like medicine and engineering, is a set of practical activities and we understand better how to carry them out if we understand the natural laws that apply to the material with which we have to work. Indeed, if we were quite ignorant of these laws, the limits of our successful practice would be very narrow. But some of the regularities of nature are much more easily known than others. Men lived successfully for many thousands of years and developed great civilizations without more than a very superficial acquaintance with the laws of mechanics and without knowing anything at all of electro-magnetism, chemistry or physiology. The laws of these sciences are not to be grasped by casual observers. Mere observation, however careful and persistent, is not enough. It needs patient and orderly *experiment* in order to make any headway at all in these fields.

That is to say, observations must be made under conditions controlled and systematically varied by the observer and directed by his hypotheses. Such sciences also require techniques of accurate measurement and devices for extending the normal reach of observation, microscopes, galvanometers, spectrographs and the like. Thus they can develop only gradually and in a civilization that puts a high value on this sort of knowledge.

But it is, to some extent, quite different in the sciences of man. One of the reasons why psychology, economics, sociology and the rest of the studies that we call social sciences developed so late is, paradoxically, just that we can learn a good deal about them by casual observation, provided that it is intelligent and critical. The rough regularities of behaviour and experience that we can all notice in ourselves, our friends and our animals are sufficient to give us all a modest stock of psychological knowledge. We know roughly how we learn, how we are motivated, how our emotions work and so on. Such knowledge is very limited, inaccurate and unorganized but it is sufficient to enable us to live our lives more or less successfully in contact with other people. So too with the other social sciences. As long as social and economic organization remains at a fairly elementary level, we can understand the operation of social and economic laws well enough to keep our institutions in control. When there is an economic crisis in a South Pacific island it is likely to be due to something obvious and inevitable like a crop failure rather than to some unexpected outcome of government policy or the defects of the monetary system.

There is thus an important difference between the laws of nature and the laws of human nature. The regularities of human and animal behaviour are clear in rough outline to an intelligent observer. But the regularities of nature lie, for the most part, beneath the surface of things and have to be painfully elucidated by the standard methods of science. This is one of the reasons why education has been a successful enterprise for many thousands of years while medicine and engineering have only recently attained maturity. A good teacher knows enough of the workings of human nature from common experience to enable him to teach effectively.

Considerations of this sort are sometimes used to discredit the social sciences and in particular, the science of psychology. But I certainly do not wish to suggest that the sciences of man are unimportant or trivial. Indeed it is just because they seem so obvious at their superficial levels that it is easy to be dangerously complacent or dogmatic about our supposed knowledge of ourselves. The accounts of human nature in educational theory from Plato to Froebel are a good example of the dangers of relying on pre-scientific psychology for our beliefs about man. Although intelligent reflection on a wide experience may give us the capacity for successful day-to-day dealings with our fellows, it will certainly not suffice for all the social occasions of a complex modern society. In just the same way, a shrewd business sense that might make a man wealthy in ancient Athens or the Solomon Islands would not be a substitute for the specialist knowledge needed by an economic adviser to the Treasury.

There is a sense in which the development of the sciences of man, like that of the natural sciences, has been determined by social conditions. The rise of modern psychology, economics and sociology has been helped by the fact that social organization has grown so complicated in the last hundred years that our rule of thumb, commonsense knowledge of man has proved quite inadequate. A very intricate economic organization will easily get out of control unless the forces at work in it are understood. Thus modern economic theory has been in part a response to the demands of an increasingly complex economy. So also modern psychological theory has arisen, partly at least, to meet the requirements of administrators for whom the problems offered by industry, mental health and education were rapidly outgrowing the crude psychological opinions common to intelligent men.

It is easy to see how this has happened in the case of education. There is no reason to suppose that the average effectiveness of the teaching given in ancient or medieval times was very much less than that of our present-day schools. No doubt, the teachers of those days used methods that would nowadays be recognized as time-wasting and inefficient but by and large they achieved their aims, such as they were. And when we look at the Greek or medieval achievements in art, literature and philosophy, it certainly does not become us, as twentieth-century critics, to despise the educational systems that furthered them. Yet it is obvious that those educational methods would not give the results that we look for today. Ancient and medieval teachers could afford to rely on traditional commonsense methods of teaching because the material on which they had to work was a small body of students selected by rank or talent. Modern education, on the other hand, is given indiscriminately to the whole of the child population. Moreover, while the teacher in former times had only to impart a limited body of knowledge and skill, modern teachers have somehow between them to ensure that the whole of contemporary knowledge is transmitted at least to sufficient numbers of students to guarantee that it will be preserved and furthered. They have also to see that practically everyone, however ill-suited by capacity or interest, can read and write sufficiently to fill up forms and understand official instructions. (Illiteracy is not, as is often pretended, a cultural problem; but it can be a serious social problem in a complex modern society.)

Thus two of the basic aims of education nowadays require that educational methods shall be as efficient as possible. For this purpose, it is necessary that what we know of the sciences of man shall be applied to ensure this increased efficiency. Thus the analogy between education and applied skills like medicine or engineering is imperfect. Even to be efficient on a small scale, medicine and engineering must be based on natural science. But education demands this only when it has so increased in scale and complexity that the laws of human nature that are patent to intelligent observers prove an inadequate theoretical basis and need to be supplemented or replaced by the sciences of man.

97

II

Before we consider the extent to which these sciences are applied in educational theory and practice, it will be useful to look at the ways in which the social sciences are supposed to differ from the natural sciences. For we have based the discussion of theories and explanation in the previous chapter on the ways in which these concepts occur in the natural sciences. We did so because sciences like physics, chemistry and astronomy are the standard cases of well-developed sciences so that the clearest and best established uses of terms like 'theory' and 'explanation' will be found there. Now we want to know how far the uses of these terms in education conform to these standard uses and how far they are weakened and derivative.

In the first place, it is well to remember that the history of the social sciences is a short one. Psychology as an experimental science has a history of less than a hundred years. Previously it had been a branch of speculative philosophy. We cannot foresee at this date how far it may progress in the future. Possibly our present-day psychology, like chemistry in the early nineteenth century, is on the threshold of a spectacular period of progress. But it may be that the subject matter of psychology and its methods can never give us this sort of systematic development. Only the future history of the science can tell us that. What we can do is to look at the sort of differences that obviously exist at present between psychology and the other sciences of man on the one hand and the sciences of nature on the other.

We must not start however by making too sharp a division between the sciences of man and the sciences of nature. Man is a part of nature. His body is as much subject as are the other parts of nature to the laws of physics, chemistry and biology. And if we look at the relations between the sciences, we do not find that there is any sharp discontinuity between the sciences peculiar to man and those common to man and the rest of nature. The laws of physics set the framework within which the laws of chemistry may be found. Chemistry sets a similar framework for biology and biology for psychology. In the same way, the laws of psychology are the limits within which the specialized sciences of man, economics, sociology and the rest can be understood. Thus the sciences can be regarded as having the same sort of relation to each other as the members of a set of Chinese boxes, the more general and abstract studies setting the limits for the more specialized. In this way there is a clear continuity between the sciences of man and the sciences of nature, just as there is a clear continuity between man himself and the rest of the universe. But having recognized this continuity, it is helpful in trying to understand the nature of theories about man, to trace whatever differences there may be between the social and the natural sciences.

The most obvious of these differences is the one I have referred to already: the main laws of the sciences of man are more obvious or at least less surprising than those of the sciences of nature. Indeed, the social sciences might be satirically defined as those sciences which tell us nothing that we do not know already. This description, in spite of being a rhetorical exaggeration, is not entirely misleading. Being men, we have every opportunity for observing the main trends of human experience and behaviour. And living in societies, we have a privileged viewpoint on the workings of societies. This inside knowledge of the subject matter of the social sciences has both advantages and drawbacks. Although it gives us some sort of rough and ready knowledge of the uniformities of human behaviour, it inhibits us from looking at them with the objective eye that the scientist needs. Moreover it is liable to make us complacent about the value and range of our common understanding of man. The layman is more suspicious of the psychologist than he is of other scientists just because he is unwilling to believe that the knowledge of man can be an intellectual speciality.

The extent to which psychology, to take only one example, conforms to this satirical description of a social science[1] may be

[1] The obvious exception to this rule seems to be social anthropology. Here we learn a great deal that is surprising and

99

tested by reading any standard elementary text-book on the subject. Those psychological discoveries that come as a surprise to us will be found, in general, to come from two different sources. Either they originate from the laboratory of the physiologist and so are not, properly speaking, part of psychology at all, or they come from the speculations of the psychiatrists. And these, however surprising they may be, are supported by such flimsy evidence that they can hardly rank as scientific discoveries.[1] Yet in spite of this, psychology is not a negligible collection of truisms in a scientific guise. It is an important and rapidly developing science with rewarding applications in many different fields. What is the explanation of this apparent contradiction?

In so far as psychology merely confirms common human opinion on man's nature, it serves three important scientific ends. In the first place, it makes this common knowledge *precise*. Secondly, it gives us an orderly account of the *evidence* for it. Our common knowledge of human nature is both vague and unsupported by adequate evidence and so cannot really rank as *knowledge* at all. It should rather be called belief or opinion. And opinions of this ill-defined and ill-supported kind cannot be reliably applied. Thirdly, the experimental psychologist can often show how the different ways in which we behave can be related together. He can thus *systematize* common opinion on these matters which in its ordinary forms tends to be piecemeal and unorganized. Thus psychology introduces into our everyday knowledge of human nature the characteristically scientific notes of precision, evidence and system and so justifies its claim to be the science of experience and be-

---

strange about the customs of men in societies very different from our own. But these surprising facts are the *material* of the anthropologist not his *conclusions*. They do however illustrate the tendency of human behaviour to take on different forms in different circumstances. This point is referred to below.

[1] For a useful critical discussion of the evidence for psychotherapy, see H. J. Eysenck, *Uses and Abuses of Psychology*, Chapter 10, and D. O. Hebb, *Organization of Behavior*, Chapter 10.

haviour. I have chosen to speak of psychology here as it is the science most clearly germane to education. But the same sort of advance from commonsense opinion to scientific knowledge occurs in the other social sciences.

There is a second obvious way in which the laws of the sciences of man differ from those of the sciences of nature. We regard the laws of nature as permanent and immutable features of the world, the same today as they were in the Old Stone Age. We have indeed no conclusive proof that they never will alter in the future or that they never have done so in the past. But we have good evidence for supposing that such variations, if they occur at all, are so slight or so infrequent as not to demand that we take account of them. But this is not quite the position with the sciences of man. The question 'Can we change human nature?' as it is popularly asked is a vague one. But it can be put in a form that is in principle capable of being answered by observational evidence, though the evidence might be very difficult to obtain. For our purposes, however, the interesting feature of the question is that it is not obviously absurd. We should never think of asking 'Can we change the laws of chemistry?'

There are several ways in which the laws of human nature might seem to be changeable. Because the sciences of man lie, as it were, in a matrix of non-human sciences, the laws of human nature depend to a largely unknown degree on the laws of physics, chemistry and biology. These sciences might therefore be applied to alter human nature as we know it. For example, applications of genetics to human breeding might conceivably alter man to the extent that wheat or maize has been altered by systematic plant-breeding. Or mutations might be induced in men, accidentally or by design, which might bring entirely new hereditary characters to mankind. The possibilities of this sort are numerous but so far, perhaps fortunately, they have been exploited only in imagination by the writers of utopian novels or science fiction. (Aldous Huxley's *Brave New World* is the best known example.) Such genetic changes, if they occurred, would tend to bring about changes in social structure. For example, systems of representative democracy as we know them are possible only because the native abilities of mankind are distributed as they are. A society in which 95 per cent of the population were mentally defective and 5 per cent of high intellectual gifts would not be a representative democracy. (It would far more probably be a slave state.)

Just as innate human tendencies have an influence on the structure of society, so social structure can influence the ways in which our hereditary capacities develop and show themselves in action. An important justification of large scale educational reforms is precisely the reasonable hope that altered social conditions will bring out features of human nature which are masked or discouraged by other kinds of educational organization.

Of course, in neither of these two cases could we properly say that the *laws* of human nature had altered. It would be rather that man, like any other part of nature, responds differently to different conditions and by altering the conditions we can provide new occasions in which previously hidden capabilities can be developed.

The extent to which we can do this points to a third difference between the natural and the social sciences. The scope of experiment is greatly limited in the social sciences. There are two main reasons for this. The first is a matter of morals. When we experiment with human material, the varying conditions to which we subject our material are restricted by the welfare of the human beings on whom we are working and by what we recognize to be their rights. In the second place, it is technically very difficult for obvious reasons to vary social conditions on any large scale. Thus the possibility of observation under controlled conditions is naturally restricted in the sciences of man. We are therefore compelled to rely largely on *comparing* what we can observe under conditions familiar to us with what we can observe under rare or unfamiliar conditions. We compare the behaviour of normal adults with that of children, savages or psychotics, or the structure of our own social system with that of societies very different from our own. This will tell us something but it is naturally much less effective than systematic experiment would be, were this possible.

Perhaps the most important of the differences between the natural and the social sciences lies in their respective levels of development. T. H. Huxley, the great Victorian biologist, suggested a very useful analysis of the development of a science into three stages. The first stage is shown at the level of commonsense knowledge of a subject as, for example, the ordinary man's casual knowledge of plants. The second stage is that of natural history exemplified by, say, the amateur botanist who finds the collection and classification of plants an interesting pastime. The third stage of a fully developed science is reached when the whole of the plant world and its environment is understood by the biologist as a complex system of interacting causes and effects. These three phases are not, of course, sharply distinct and the third stage of any science is never completely achieved. Natural history, the second stage, is the descriptive and classificatory phase of a science. It falls roughly into two parts: (*a*) careful and exact observation and recording of facts; (*b*) the intelligent classification of these facts to reduce them to a manageable and comprehensible order. The social sciences are, for the most part, in this second phase of development and in some of them development has not gone far enough for us to know if the third stage will ever be possible. Social science in its present state is little more than the natural history of man.

These are the most important differences between the natural and the social sciences.[1] We can point also to others

---

[1] It is sometimes claimed by writers on the methodology of the social sciences that the question of 'free will' and the problem of value judgments present peculiar difficulties for the social scientist. These are old fallacies which are unfortunately still believed by some. I mention them here only for this reason. 'Free will' presents a philosophical problem which has no bearing on factual question of how far the *statistical* predictions of the social scientists are reliable. And though value judgments may form part of the social scientist's *material*, they do not, if he

in techniques of measurement, in the precision with which the technical terms of the science can be defined, in the kinds of explanation used,[1] in the degree to which theories can be systematized; and so on. Some of these differences are due to the nature of the material with which the scientist has to work and some of them are due to the stage of development that the science has reached. Only the future development of the sciences can tell us how fundamental these differences are. But in considering the status of educational theories we have to take the social sciences as they are at present.

III

I now come to the main question with which this chapter is concerned: How far should educational theories properly be called 'theories'? And what kind of theories are they? I suppose that it will have been obvious from what was said earlier that theories in education do not, in general, conform to the models that we find in a well-developed natural science. We have discussed very briefly some of the reasons for this. Nevertheless, it would be absurd to deny that education has a theoretical basis. What we should be clear about however is what job these educational theories do if they do not have the logical status of standard scientific theories.

If we read a text-book on educational theories or the history of educational ideas, we can find three quite different sorts of statement which have been put forward as a basis for educational practice.[2] These kinds of statement are different in the sense that they belong to distinct logical families and for that

---

is a good scientist, influence his *conclusions*. They may, of course, affect the methods he adopts but no more so than they may affect the methods of the chemist or the biologist. (See page 102 above.)

[1] See Chapter 4 above, pages 90–91.
[2] It is a useful elementary exercise in philosophical criticism to read some standard texts on education with the object of detecting the different kinds of statement which occur there. On the whole, the better the writing, the easier it will be to recognize its different components.

reason need to be supported in quite different ways. Often indeed we find that the three kinds are mixed up together in the writings of a single man so that it is not easy to judge the value of what he is saying until we have distinguished the different logical components and evaluated them separately. First, there is often a *metaphysical* part to educational writings. This occurs most obviously in the writings of Plato and the medieval scholastics and, in modern times, in the educational theories of Christian writers. Statements of this kind are not believed, in the first place, just because they form part of an educational theory. They are accepted rather because they feature in a philosophy or a theology which is already believed on other grounds. But they occur in educational writings naturally enough because they are the sort of statements which seem to have an important bearing on education. Many of Plato's educational proposals, for example, are based on the beliefs that man is essentially a soul or spirit in a temporary association with a material body, that this soul was created before the body and will survive its dissolution and that the real object of education is 'improvement of the soul'. This belief in a radical distinction between soul and body is, of course, a metaphysical one. It has never been demonstrated by any recognized process of argument. Nor can we even be sure what sort of argument could establish it. Christianity took over from Platonism this belief in an immaterial and immortal soul in a temporary relation with a material and corruptible body. And it has added a more precise and circumstantial account than Plato's of the divine origin of souls and their destiny. Moreover, it has supplemented this with an explanation of the relation of man to God in terms of the doctrines of the incarnation, grace and salvation. Whether true or false, all of these doctrines, Platonic and Christian alike, are metaphysical in the sense in which we have understood this word. Nevertheless, they have had an enormous influence on the aims and methods of education. And it is easy to see why this has been so. If we hold that every human being is an immortal soul, created by God for an eternal destiny and placed here on earth in a state of probation, this belief has an important effect on the aims and content of the educational system that we shall be prepared to support.[1] We have seen that the main difficulty about claims of this kind is that there is no well-established way of confirming them. It is therefore impossible to say exactly what is being claimed or even to be sure that such statements have any cognitive meaning at all. Propositions of this kind do not always show their character on their faces. But they may usually be recognized because however much they may look like ordinary statements of fact, they are basically unlike them in at least one way: they cannot either be confirmed or refuted by evidence which can be collected, checked and assessed by established and publicly recognized methods. It is important that, whether or not we suppose that such statements are meaningful or provable, we should at least be able to recognize them. For it is hardly possible to understand them if we do not appreciate their logical status.

The second type of statement embodied in educational theories consists of *judgments of value*. These are inevitable in

---

[1] The following point is important but is put here in a footnote because it may be found difficult. It is not possible to deduce statements about the aims of a system of education or its curriculum from any purely *philosophical* statements. This follows from an obvious extension of Hume's principle which we discussed in Chapter 3, namely, that the evidence for any conclusion must contain statements of the same logical sort as the conclusion itself. There is a sense in which a practical policy for education can 'follow from' a psychological theory about human motivation, for example, or the learning process. But it does not follow from it in any logical sense. It is merely that if we know or think that we know something about the motives governing human conduct, it would be foolish not to take advantage of this knowledge in planning the educational system just as it would be foolish not to use our knowledge of hydrostatics in designing a system of plumbing. In a similar way, philosophical statements *which are metaphysical* can have practical consequences for education *just because such statements purport to be factual as well as philosophical*. The difficulty, as we have seen, is that these 'facts' are of a peculiarly inaccessible kind. This point is of considerable importance for the philosophy of education.

any system of education, though they are sometimes disguised so that the very proponents of an educational system may be imperfectly aware of the values that guide their practice. Part of the use of philosophical criticism of an educational theory is to dissect out and make plain its guiding values. Most of the catchwords and slogans of the educational reformer are fossilized value judgments: 'education according to nature', 'education for democracy', 'equality of opportunity', 'education for citizenship' and the rest. It is of the greatest importance that directives of this sort should not remain mere slogans. They should be explicitly formulated, related to practice and *recognized for what they are*. An undiagnosed value judgment is a source of intellectual muddle. Once we recognize it, we realize that it is not 'self evidently true' and beyond all criticism. For however important and inevitable our valuations are, we have seen that their justification is a very perplexing philosophical problem. If we realize this we shall tend not to be dogmatic or fanatical about them.

The third component of educational theories is *empirical*, being capable of being supported by the evidence of observable fact. Empirical components of educational theories are, in general, of two different kinds. The first of these is relatively common in the writings of those theorists who lived before psychology became established as an experimental science. They consist of recommendations for educational practice. These recommendations may of course be made on theoretical grounds but they have been adopted rather because of their efficiency in giving results. The influence of educational reformers like Pestalozzi, Froebel and Montessori is due more to their precepts and their practical achievements than to their theoretical teachings. A new practical approach to teaching is more influential than a new theory about teaching. Ideally of course a new technique should be capable of being justified by theoretical considerations as it usually is in engineering or medicine, just as a new theory, if it is genuinely a theory, should result in practical advantages when it is applied in the classroom. But we do not find that the connexion between most educational theories and their practice is as close as this. It is rather similar in this respect to the present state of psycho-therapy where there are a number of different therapeutic techniques in use, each with its theoretical background. It is found that although the theories are incompatible with one another, the techniques as used by skilled practitioners all seem to produce sufficient results to justify their continued use. And this would be impossible if the techniques were in fact tied as closely to their supposed theoretical foundation as is the case with physical or chemical theory and its applications. We must rather suppose that the theories of the psychiatrists are rationalizations of their practice rather than genuine reasons for them.

The same seems to be true of much of the so-called theory underlying established educational practice. The fact that a well conducted school using the Dalton plan or Montessori or Froebel methods produces good results is, of itself, no justi-fication whatever of the supposed theoretical background of these practices. If indeed a representative group of schools using, say, project methods of teaching consistently got better results than a comparable group of schools using other methods, that would be some evidence in favour of Dewey's educational theories which the project method was designed to apply. But no very convincing evidence of this sort seems to be available at present.[1] The cumulative effect of new proposals for teaching techniques is of course considerable over long periods of time. The teaching practice and curriculum of a present-day primary school is very different from those of a similar school of seventy years ago. And these differences are due to the ingenuity and hard work of many educational reformers. But the adoption of these different improvements in the art of teaching does not commit anyone to adopting the often elaborate 'theoretical' justifications of the new methods. The introduction of a new

[1] For recent work of this kind, see the references cited by W. D. Wall in his lecture *Teaching Methods: Psychological Studies of the Curriculum and of Classroom Teaching* in University of London Institute of Education Studies in Education No. 7.

teaching method has often been more like the empirical insight
of a herbalist in the early stages of medicine. Practice comes
first; but its theoretical justification has to wait for the scientific
development that can explain its success. Thus educational
theories which preceded the rise of a scientific psychology
(when they were not metaphysical speculations or ethical judgments) were more or less acute guesses at explaining successful
practice. Some of them were acute and systematic but mistaken like the psychology of Herbart.[1] Some were unsub-
stantiated conjectures, like Montessori's views on the training
of the senses. Some, like Pestalozzi's doctrine of *Anschauung*,
were unintelligible adaptations of metaphysical concepts.
Many of such theorists indeed seem to have taken to heart the
rule of method by which Rousseau attempted to explain the
nature of man: 'Let us then begin by laying facts aside, as they
do not affect the question.' It is not therefore surprising that
the results were unsatisfactory. Usually however these abortive
theories were just glosses on fruitful innovations in educational
practice. It was the practice that mattered.

But the development of a scientific psychology has put us in
the position where we no longer have to rely on practice to
suggest theory. It may, of course, still do so but it is *experiment*
rather than practice which now suggests theory. The relationship between theory and practice has become a reciprocal one.
Theory directs practice and practice corrects theory. Present-
day knowledge of perception, learning, motivation, the nature
of 'intelligence' and its distribution and development, the
causes of educational backwardness, and many other matters of
this kind enable us to amend educational practice in the ex-
pectation of improved results. We have, in other words, a body
of established hypotheses that have been confirmed to a
reliable degree. They enable us to predict the outcome of their
application and to explain the processes that we are trying to
control. They are, to that extent, genuine theories in the

[1] For a good example of philosophical criticism of a standard
'educational theory', see C. D. Hardie's analysis of Herbart in
Truth and Fallacy in Educational Theory.

standard scientific sense of the word. Even so, they do not approach the theories of the physical sciences in their explanatory power. For example, learning theory is one of the best developed fields of psychology. The processes of human and animal learning have been very thoroughly studied by experimental methods for over fifty years. The great mass of accumulated results of this work has greatly improved our understanding of how we learn but it has not yet been condensed into a single overall theory. There are several theories of learning all of which seem to be compatible with most of the known facts without being necessitated by them. No one of them fits the facts so perfectly as to exclude all its rivals. What are still needed are crucial experiments which will enable the psychologists to decide between one theory and another.[1] Thus even the best examples of theories in the sciences of man are less closely tied to their supporting facts than theories in the sciences of nature.

We can summarize this discussion by saying that the word 'theory' as it is used in educational contexts is generally a courtesy title. It is justified only where we are applying well-established experimental findings in psychology or sociology to the practice of education. And even here we should be aware that the conjectural gap between our theories and the facts on which they rest is sufficiently wide to make our logical consciences uneasy. We can hope that the future development of the social sciences will narrow this gap and this hope gives an incentive for developing these sciences.

[1] For an excellent account of the relation of contemporary learning theory to education, see R. W. Russell, *How Children Learn*, in University of London Institute of Education Studies in Education No. 7.

6

SOME QUESTIONS OF MORALS AND RELIGION

I

THE connexions between philosophy and education that I have discussed so far have given the philosopher the role of a critic rather than that of a discoverer. This will seem unsatisfactory to those who believe that philosophy can give some positive guidance to educational theorists and can therefore have more than the modest regulative task that I have tried to describe. I have explained in Chapters 2 and 3 some of the reasons for supposing that the task of philosophy in relation to education is as I have stated it. Nevertheless this question is a fundamental one and needs more than the merely incidental treatment it has received up to now. I shall therefore discuss in this final chapter some of the philosophical issues basic to any educational theory.

It is worth pointing out, before we go on to discuss the claims of philosophy to be able to make a positive contribution to educational theory, that the outcome of philosophizing conceived as a process of analysis and criticism is not merely negative and destructive. The critical philosopher is not to be thought of as a sort of intellectual demolition contractor who sweeps away the constructive work of others and leaves nothing in its place. He is rather, in one of his roles at least, a sort of inspector or assayer who rejects those theories and arguments which can be shown to be faulty by the logical touchstones or gauges which are his stock in trade. Nor is this work of assessment the whole of critical philosophy. A large and important part of it consists in trying to provide the *analysis* of concepts like 'cause', 'self', 'mind', 'voluntary action', 'obligation', 'good', 'society' and so on, concepts which play a central part in our scientific, moral and political thinking. It is hoped that the outcome of this clarificatory activity will be to reveal logical tangles in these concepts and in their relations to their neighbours. It will then often be possible to remove these sources of confusion by remodelling the concepts. Finally, the critical philosopher cannot claim to be innocent of theory-making. In his criticism of the philosophical theories of his contemporaries and predecessors he is led often enough to a reformulation of these theories rather than to a total rejection of them. Sometimes indeed he constructs theories of his own, though such theories tend to be interpretations of experience *in terms of experience* and not like the theories of the metaphysical philosophers in terms of entities transcending experience. Philosophical theory construction when it is undertaken by critical philosophers is in the nature of a reshuffling of the items of experience into a comprehensible pattern like the solution of a jigsaw puzzle. This is very unlike traditional metaphysics which often invoked unknown and unknowable entities or arbitrary 'principles' to account for our puzzlement about the everyday world.

Nevertheless, though the work of those philosophers who are called 'critical empiricists' or 'logical analysts' is in a sense constructive as well as critical, it does not give us any new knowledge as does the work of the scientist. Rather it gives us a new point of view on what we already know and so may properly be said to provide understanding rather than knowledge. By reformulating and reinterpreting the common content of human experience it tries to provide the same sort of unifying overall views of experience as traditional metaphysical systems purported to supply. But since it tries to do this without going beyond experience, it does not pretend to add to our knowledge of the world. There are thus three main parts to the work of the critical or analytic philosopher. He can act in a purely critical capacity in correcting or refuting the theories of other philosophers. He can trace the logical inter-connexions of certain crucial concepts which experience has shown to be the centres of philosophical disputes and puzzles. In doing so he can hope to trace some of these puzzles to their sources. Finally he can construct philosophical theories to systematize and elucidate human experience provided that in doing so he does not indulge in those transcendental extrava-gances of metaphysics that have been shown by the history of philosophy to be ineffective.[1] The outcome of philosophizing according to this programme is twofold. It has the negative effect of an intellectual antiseptic, inhibiting the growth of concepts and theories that lie beyond the common check of logic and experience. It can have also the positive result of clarifying and refocusing our thinking on those questions that we find puzzling and for which the growth of natural knowledge gives no final solutions. Such are the questions of morality, politics, religion and education.

But these negative virtues of clarity, order and intellectual antisepsis do not impress everyone. The word 'philosophy' promises much more than this to many people. And how can we be sure that this promise cannot be honoured? The best reason for being sure about this has been given more than once in the previous chapters. It is simply that some of the ablest men have done their best during twenty-five centuries to work out metaphysical views of the universe and man's place in it which would provide a positive answer to these disputed questions of religion and morality and have all failed.[2] By saying that

[1] Examples of constructive philosophical thinking by contem-porary philosophers of very different outlooks can be seen in Reichenbach's *Experience and Prediction*, Ryle's *Concept of Mind*, Price's *Thinking and Experience*, Goodman's *Structure of Appear-ance* or Körner's *Conceptual Thinking*.

[2] Some metaphysicians have been driven to desperate exped-ients in order to explain that their theories about religion and morality have not found general acceptance. For example, the

they have failed, I mean that none of their proposed solutions of these problems has stood up to criticism and been found acceptable to the majority of experts in the same field. We have the same reason for rejecting metaphysics as we have for rejecting witchcraft, astrology or phrenology: it cannot do what it claims to do. There is of course the bare possibility that the true metaphysical system has not yet been discovered just as it is barely possible that the right method of casting effective spells or veridical horoscopes has not yet been found. But this bare possibility need not raise more than an academic doubt. For we have positive grounds in the recent development of philosophy for rejecting the grandiose claims of metaphysics just as we have positive grounds in the development of natural science for judging the truth of witchcraft or astrology to be fantastically improbable.

I have done no more in previous chapters than sketch in very rough outline, what these grounds are. This rough outline was given in the discussion on the use of reason and the nature of genuine questions in Chapter 2. It would need a book on the theory of knowledge to justify this point of view in detail.[1] We can however look briefly at some particular ways in which the claim of metaphysics are sometimes stated in order to have some idea at least why the claim should be accepted with reserve. I shall therefore examine first some metaphysical questions that seem at first sight to have a close bearing on the basic problems of education. I shall then consider what relevance, if any, religion has to educational theory.

Roman Catholic apologist Jacques Maritain explains that his moral theory has been rejected 'not because of any weakness in objective proof but because of the weakness inherent in human minds' (*Education at the Crossroads*, p. 7). I have not met any other instances of a philosopher explaining the rejection of his theory by the stupidity of all his critics. But once it is assumed that philosophers can *prove* their theories, this explanation seems natural enough.

[1] See the Bibliographical Note to Chapter 2.

II

In an interesting paper on the aims of education,[1] Professor E. B. Castle quotes a statement of the Roman Catholic philosopher Jacques Maritain that all philosophical thinking begins with three simple questions: 'What are we?' 'Where are we?' and 'Where ought we to be going?' These questions certainly have been asked by philosophers and are indeed still asked by those among them for whom philosophizing means giving an intellectual justification of a particular theological system. These questions are moreover regarded as characteristically philosophical by many educated laymen because they seem to have a ring of profundity in them. To ask 'What am I?' or Where am I?' in this metaphysical tone of voice sounds impressive. And it sounds very different indeed from the question 'Where am I?' asked by someone who is lost in the country or is returning to consciousness after an accident; or the question 'What am I?' asked in a children's charade. It may be helpful in trying to understand the limits of philosophy if we look more closely at Maritain's supposed philosophical questions.

The third of them, 'Where ought we to be going?', need not detain us. Translated from its metaphorical form, the question presumably means: 'What ought to be our aim in life?' And this is merely a variant of those ethical questions of value that we discussed in Chapter 3. The other questions are more puzzling.

If anyone asks these questions in their 'profound' sense it will be no use at all to give him an answer in terms of established facts. If a man says to you, in this metaphysical accent, 'What am I?' it will be useless to reply: 'You are a human being brought up in English middle-class society in the twentieth century . . .' and so on. You could certainly give him a very full answer by offering a general description of human beings in the language of biology and psychology and a particular description of the questioner in terms of his heredity and life history. But such an answer, however detailed and exact it

[1] *Hibbert Journal*, March 1955.

might be, would be rejected by your questioner as inadequate and indeed, as irrelevant. Similarly if he asks 'Where am I?' it will be pointless to reply in terms of geography and astronomy. The questioner knows, in other words, that it is not that kind of answer that he is looking for. But does he also know what kind of an answer he *is* expecting? We have already seen that it is essential that he should know this if his question is to be a real one.

We might be inclined to say: 'Of course, he must know this. For if he did not, he could not reject as irrelevant the answers that we gave him.' But we must not assume too hastily that this shows that such questions are genuine and straightforward requests for enlightenment. A question may be a pseudo-question in more than one way. It may fail, as we have seen, by setting *no* limits within which the answer has to fall or by setting them far too widely. But it may also fail to be genuine by setting the limits too exactly. If a teacher asks a pupil 'What is three times seventeen?' or 'What is the dative plural of *canis*?' these are not genuine questions. For the teacher knows the answers already and would not accept any answers but 'fifty-one' to the first question and '*canibus*' to the second. Such questions are designed not to abate the questioner's ignorance but to test the respondent's knowledge.

Now instances of Maritain's metaphysical queries are often very similar to this. The questioner wants to hear an answer of the following kind: 'You are a finite creature, created by God and dependent on him', or 'You are here in this temporal state as a probationer to prove your fitness for eternal life', or something of this familiar sort. Such questions may be asked of someone in order to elicit his beliefs but it is true that such questions are not usually put as by a teacher to a pupil. More commonly the questioner wants his respondent to give him a certain sort of answer as a sympathetic response and an emotional reassurance, or the question may be merely a rhetorical one. However that may be, he will probably reject not only factual naturalistic answers such as those given above, but even alternative metaphysical answers. For instance, if we say to him: 'You are just a fortuitous concourse of atoms' he would reject this also. If therefore the questioner expects answers of this very specific kind and shows his expectations by rejecting any other answers, he is not putting a genuine question. For precisely this reason, such questions cannot serve as a *starting point*, as Maritain suggests, for philosophical discussions. For these are disguised *conclusions* of arguments on natural religion and very debatable conclusions at that.

Often however the man who asks such questions and shows himself dissatisfied with naturalistic answers to them is asking an empty question for the opposite reason which we met before. He has no idea at all of how the questions are to be answered beyond feeling a vague and unformulated dissatisfaction with replies in terms of scientific description and historical fact. And to such a questioner we must put the cautionary challenge 'What sort of an answer *would* satisfy you?' Thus the questions which Maritain and many other speculators in his fashion claim to be the direction finders for basic philosophical thinking turn out on examination to be either affirmations of a very specific kind of religious faith, misleadingly expressed, or a premature expression of puzzlement before an unformulated question. Nevertheless it is useful to examine them here not only because they are often put forward as genuine and profound problems but also because they raise a very important question that we have not so far considered. This is the question of the place of religion in determining the basic aims of living and so, indirectly the basic ends of education.

It may be thought absurd to try to examine so considerable and controversial a question in the course of a few pages. Yet the basic issues are very simple and they can easily be stated in quite a summary form. The passionate disputes that centre about this question are, as might be expected, quite unconnected with the logical points on which the answer to it depends. It is well known that men do not dispute passionately over points of logic. We can state the orthodox view on this matter as follows: 'Education is a training given to young people to enable them to live their lives usefully and happily.

Part of this training must be practical and utilitarian such as imparting basic skills and training them for their vocations. But the more important part of it must be designed to teach them to live in a wider sense than merely taking their place in society and earning their living. It must teach them the end or purpose of life itself; for only by showing this can we go beyond the mundane questions of finding the right means to the ends set by our desires. Only if we show how desires themselves should be directed and the ends of our actions fixed can education claim to be complete. And this sort of knowledge is religious knowledge. For only religion can decide these basic questions.'

There are two questions to be considered:

(i) Can religion tell us the 'purpose of life' or the 'meaning of existence'?
(ii) Is there any connexion between morality and religion and, if so, what sort of connexion is it?

The first question is closely allied to Maritain's metaphysical questions. I shall therefore look at it before considering the connexions between morals and religion.

III

It is claimed by many people that religion gives human existence a direction and a purpose that nothing else can give. As long as men go on asking for 'the meaning of life' or 'the purpose of man' religion alone can give them the answer. And it is these questions that lie at the basis of any theory of education. It is worth while looking closely at this claim as this is a point at which not only religion but philosophy also is often invoked. And indeed a little philosophical analysis can show what these questions are worth and how, if at all, they are to be answered. The question 'What is the purpose of X?' can be used with several different meanings. One of these is appropriate when the X refers to a conscious individual, a man for example or an animal; a second is used when the X refers to an inanimate object, usually some artefact. If I ask 'What was his

purpose in changing his job?' I expect to be told that he wanted
to earn more money or to find more congenial work or to get
more spare time or something of this sort. In other words, I
expect an answer in terms of the motives and intentions of the
X into whose purpose I am enquiring. If however I ask 'What
is the purpose of this piece of machinery?' I expect to be told
the kind of task that the machine is designed to perform. I
expect to be told, for example, that it is designed to perform
mathematical computations or to sort eggs or to dig potatoes.
I am told not the purposes *of the machine*, for an inanimate
thing has no purposes in the literal sense, but the purposes
of its designer. This distinction is obvious enough but it is
commonly overlooked in so-called philosophical discussions
about the purpose of living.

If then we ask: 'What is the purpose of man?' we can expect
at least two different kinds of answer. The most obvious type
of answer to this question is to say: 'Man has many purposes,
to keep alive, to find food and shelter, to seek virtue and
knowledge, to attain happiness, and so on.' There is no limit
to the list that might be given. But this would be an answer
to the question taken in the first of the two senses that I have
distinguished. The questioner might well reply: 'Yes, of course,
I know that those are some of men's purposes but what I want
to know is: *What is man for?*'

Now this looks superficially like asking the question in the
second of the two senses. But the second sense is ordinarily used
only when the X into whose purposes we are enquiring is an
inanimate object and, usually, an artefact *which we know, on
other grounds, to be designed for a purpose*. If we ask it about
natural features of the world, we usually mean 'What is the
function of X, that is, what job does it do?' If, for instance, I
ask 'What is the purpose of a butterfly's antennae?' this is just
another way of saying 'What job do its antennae do for the
butterfly? What sort of organs are they?' But the verbal
similarity of this question to 'What is the purpose of this
machine?' makes it easy to forget that if we ask it about things
not already known to be designed and constructed for a

purpose, we are begging the important question which has first to be asked: 'Is this X designed for a purpose at all?' The basic fault of such questions as 'What is the purpose of man?' or 'What is the meaning of life?' is that they beg the more fundamental question 'Is the universe designed and created for a purpose?' Until we have evidence to ensure that the answer to this is 'Yes', we have no right to ask such questions. They merely repeat the old sophism exemplified in the question 'Have you stopped beating your wife?'

Suppose then that we do ask the question: 'Is the universe designed for a purpose?' or 'Is man designed for a purpose?', what sort of evidence should we need to answer it? This question has often been asked and answered by philosophers by an argument of the following sort. There are countless features of the natural world which show clear indications of close adaptation of means to ends. The operation of the solar system, the sense organs of animals, the pollination mechanisms of plants, and thousands of other examples of this sort are instances of adaptations which would be almost infinitely improbable if we suppose them to be the outcome of the chance operation of natural causes.[1] Moreover, we know from our own experience that adaptation of means to ends is clear evidence of intelligent planning. No one would suppose that a watch or a book or an aeroplane could possibly be produced by the chance interplay of the forces of nature. We may therefore conclude that the universe which shows so many of these adaptations is the outcome of intelligent planning and that it is the work of a designer. The purpose of the universe and, therefore, of man who is a part of the universe is thus the purpose of this designer. The name usually given to this inferred designer of the universe is 'God'. Now God's purposes can be known to us through religion, if they can be known at all. Thus only

[1] Note that 'chance' and 'purpose' are contrasted in this argument, quite unjustifiably, as if they were clear-cut terms which are known not only to be mutually exclusive but to exhaust between them all the ways in which events can be brought about. This begs the question at issue.

religion can inform us about man's purpose and the meaning of his existence.

This line of argument can be made very persuasive by suitable elaboration of the examples of adaptation of means to ends that we observe in nature. It has always been the most popular of the arguments for the existence of God since it appeals to facts well known to everyone and does not rely on any metaphysical abstractions. But it is, for all that, a very poor argument and provides no good evidence at all in favour of the world being the work of a conscious designer. In the first place, it will be seen that the basic premiss on which it depends is the statement that adaptation of means to ends is conclusive evidence of intelligent planning. If we ask what reason there is to believe this statement, we shall be told that we have the reason in our own experience. We are surrounded in our daily life with things which bear the stamp of intelligent design upon them, houses, books, telephones, machines and artefacts of all kinds on which we can base our assurance that adaptation of means to ends entails design.

But this is a very bad piece of reasoning. Suppose that it were true that all processes directed by intelligent beings involve adaptation of means to ends. It would still not follow that *all* adaptation of means to ends was the work of intelligence. At best, the argument looks like a rather weak piece of inductive reasoning from the character of a sample to the character of the population from which the sample was taken. ('All the housewives interviewed preferred X to any other detergent; therefore, *all* housewives prefer X.') But such an argument is worth considering only if we have reason to believe that the untested part of the material we are investigating is similar in relevant respects to the part we have tested. And this is just what we cannot say in the argument from design. For in this case *we could never test the rest of the material* however much we might wish to do so. That is to say, we have no possible means of applying a test for intelligent design to those phenomena which display adaptation of means to ends but are not already known *on other grounds* to be planned.

And these are precisely the cases in question; for example, brains, eyes, plants, the solar system and so on. The fallacy becomes more patent if we look more closely at the supposed evidence. If we were to dredge up a watch from the bottom of the sea, we should not hesitate to say that it had been intelligently planned and constructed. But we should say this only because we were acquainted with other instances of watches or similar artefacts and had independent evidence that they were designed and constructed by intelligent creatures. We can visit watch factories and see them being planned and made. But in the case of the supposed intelligent design shown in nature, we have no such independent evidence and can, moreover, never get any. We cannot observe the hypothetical Designer of the Universe at his task in the way in which we can observe an architect at work in his studio or a watchmaker at his bench. The human eye may be very like a camera in certain basic ways but we have independent methods for confirming that cameras are designed and none for confirming that human eyes are. The human brain has some similarity to an electronic calculator but we have not the same sort of reason for believing that it is designed as we have in the case of the calculator. In fact, we have no reason at all. For brains, eyes and the rest are unlike watches and other artefacts in a way which destroys the supposed analogy between them.

There are other equally serious criticisms that may be made of this argument but it will be sufficient for our purposes to show that there is no reason to believe its basic premiss. And if we do not accept this premiss, we have no reason to suppose that the universe or any part of it, such as man himself, is designed for a purpose. Of course, the fact that the argument is invalid does not prove that there is no purpose of this kind. It shows only that we have no reason for believing that there is. Strictly, indeed, it shows only that we cannot have *this* reason for believing in a cosmic purpose. But in the absence of any other argument, we may fairly say that we have no reason for believing that there is a purpose in the universe which is not that of the conscious agents, men and perhaps animals, who are known to have purposes. It is still open to us to interpret the word 'purpose' in the sense of 'function' as we do with the question: 'What is the purpose of a butterfly's antennae?' And to the question: 'What is the function of man?' we may indeed look for an answer in terms of physiology, psychology and the sciences of society. But for the reasons we have already considered, such answers are unlikely to satisfy anyone who asks these metaphysical questions.

Perhaps the tendency to ask these questions can be accounted for in part by the ambiguity of the words 'purpose' and 'meaning'. The phrase 'the purpose of X' may mean (*a*) the intention of the conscious individual X; (*b*) the function of X; (*c*) the intention of the conscious individual who designed X. And it is only if we interpret the phrase 'the purpose of man' in sense (*c*) that we can sensibly talk of the purpose of man. (Otherwise we should talk of the *purposes of men*.) And to do this it is necessary, as we have seen, first to show that there is a conscious individual who designed man, bearing in mind the weakness of the argument ordinarily invoked to establish this. The phrases 'the meaning of life' or 'the meaning of existence' may be clarified accordingly. The word 'meaning' here has a metaphorical sense. One who asks for the meaning of life is not asking to be told the meaning of the *word* 'life'. He wants to know the purposes or intentions that underlie or direct living. We have seen how this question is to be treated. And this, though it does not give us the answer, does give us a reason for ceasing to ask the question.

I do not wish to imply by what I have said that anyone who believes that life has a purpose beyond the purposes of the men who live it is merely deluded. A statement may be true even if we have no evidence for it. There are countless statements which can be made without evidence and which later may turn out to be true. But in such cases, simply because we have no evidence, we should be unwise to put much reliance on the statements. However, we must be careful in talking in this way about religious beliefs if we are not both to seem unfair to them and to have our criticism misunderstood. A believer may justifiably object that all this talk of reasons for belief and of logical criticism of such reasons is beside the point. He may say that the real grounds of any religious belief are not rational and that we do no service to religion if we pretend that they are. This is not to say, moreover, that such beliefs are *irrational*; they are not held in defiance of the rules by which we collect and evaluate evidence. Rather it is the case that they are non-rational; they are beliefs that do not require to be justified by such methods. We must remember Pascal's well-known saying: 'The heart has its reasons of which reason knows nothing.'

That there are such beliefs and that many (but not all) of the beliefs of religious people are of this kind is, I think, undeniable. It is obvious that the vast majority of believers in all religions neither require rational justification for their faith nor would they appreciate it, were it possible to give it to them. And though sophisticated and intellectual believers are prepared to defend or even to establish their beliefs by argument, their faith certainly does not depend on the evidence by which they seek to justify it. For it is not weakened if their arguments are refuted.

Why then do we discuss such questions as topics for philosophical criticism? The relation between faith and reason is not a matter that theologians themselves are agreed on and it would be out of place to discuss it here. But there are at least two good reasons why philosophers should look at these questions. In the first place, if anyone puts forward an argument for, say, the existence of God, he must be presumed, by the very fact that he does so, to submit himself to the rules of logic. He is understood, therefore, to be setting up his argument as a target for criticism and to agree that its logical worth shall be tested in this way. To criticize such arguments is to offer the theologians who propound them the compliment of taking them seriously. No one who offers a rational defence of his religion wishes to be understood as saying: 'If these arguments are valid, they establish my case; but if they are invalid, the rational grounds for my beliefs are unaffected.' This would indeed be the confidence trickster's policy of 'Heads I win, tails you lose.' (But here we must bear in mind that if we destroy the rational support for a proposition, we have not necessarily proved it to be false. We have merely shown it to be incapable of proof in this way.)

A second reason for the philosophical examination of the grounds for belief was given by Immanuel Kant, himself a religious man. Commenting on the tendency for certain fields of human interest, including religion, to claim exemption from rational criticism, he remarks: 'But then they awaken just suspicion and cannot claim the sincere respect which reason accords only to that which has been able to sustain the test of free and open examination.'[1]

But it would be rash to suppose that the validity of religious faith can be discredited by philosophical criticism, however successful. All that can be shown in this way is that religious beliefs do not admit of rational support and are therefore immune to rational criticism. But it is important to notice that if we claim that a statement can be supported by argument, we must be prepared to admit that, *in so far as it is a candidate for rational discussion*, it is capable, in principle, of being refuted by argument; and vice versa. We must not claim the benefits of reason without acknowledging its risks. There is no doubt that sources of belief which are grounded in faith or mystical intuition are far more compelling reasons for a believer than any arguments. But they cannot be of any concern for rational enquiry; for they cannot be either communicated or demonstrated. All that the philosopher can do is to recognize the existence and the force of such non-rational convictions and perhaps insist on the necessity of treating them with caution. For beliefs of this sort are often conflicting and of any set of conflicting statements, not more than one can be right. (Though they may all be false, they cannot all be true.) Where statements which can be supported by public evidence are in conflict, we can at least look for the evidence. But where faith or intuition give discordant directions, there is nothing

[1] Professor Kemp Smith's translation.

we can do. It is this fact, more than any other, which offers a practical justification for the philosophical scrutiny of the claims of religion.

IV

The second question that we have to consider concerns the nature of the connexion between morality and religion. The word 'religion' is a vague one and if we try to define it too closely, we may find ourselves forced to decide rather arbitrarily on the basis of our definition whether a certain set of beliefs and practices is or is not a religion. For example, may we use the term to describe those forms of Buddhism which do not recognize the existence of a God? Students of comparative religion have shown that we can usually trace three elements in those social institutions which have been called 'religions'. They commonly embody a set of moral rules, a set of observances or rituals and a set of beliefs about God or the universe and man's relation to it. In short, they embody a code, a cult and a creed. Some religions lay more emphasis on one of these elements than on another but each of them can be found in what are usually called religions, though sometimes in a rather attenuated form. A moral code was not the most important feature of ancient Greek religion nor are religious rituals highly developed in the Society of Friends. For our present purposes it is the moral code that is the important feature. What we want to know is whether an effective moral code can exist apart from a religious setting and, indeed, whether such a code has any essential connexion with religion at all. Granted that all developed religions have some sort of moral content, is the converse true that all moral codes must have some sort of a religious foundation? If we answer 'Yes' to this question, it will follow that religion is basic to education since we have seen that the judgments that direct the use of our educational means are moral judgments. How is this question to be decided?

If morality is essentially bound up with religion, it will be for one of two reasons. Either the connexion will be a *logical* one so that a man who accepted a moral code and yet rejected any form of religious belief would be adopting a self-contradictory position; or else the connexion will be a *factual* or *empirical* one. If this were the case, it would be possible for a man to hold to a set of moral rules without holding any supporting religious beliefs but such a position would then perhaps be psychologically difficult to maintain and would, for that reason, be uncommon. Those who hold that morality is impossible without religion do not usually make clear which of these alternative views they support and often perhaps they have not thought the matter out so far. Let us therefore look at each in turn.

A philosopher who holds that there is a *logical* connexion between the laws of morality and the truths of religion might put his case in several different ways. He might claim, for example, that the value statements of ethics logically imply certain statements about natural religion. It is not uncommon for people to maintain that the existence of moral obligations is itself evidence for the existence of a God. Conversely, however, it is sometimes held that we can prove the existence of a God from non-ethical premises and we can then use the existence of God and certain demonstrable facts about his nature to show that human beings are subject to a moral law. Some philosophers indeed have been willing to hold both of these views even at the cost of appearing to reason in a circle. To refute such suggestions it is not sufficient to reply that there have been plenty of intelligent and highly moral unbelievers and that it is very unlikely that intelligent men would hold a view that was not only false but logically self-contradictory. It is only too easy, as the history of mathematics shows, to hold logically inconsistent opinions where the subject matter is abstruse and difficult.

We are concerned here only with the claim that the validity of moral judgments needs to be guaranteed by the truths of religion and to this claim we have a simple and conclusive answer in Hume's famous argument that we examined in Chapter 3. Anyone who argues from statements about religion

to statements about moral values argues from premisses which
do not contain value concepts to statements which do. The
argument must therefore be invalid for the reasons we have
already considered. And if it is claimed that the value concepts
are already implicit in the religious premisses, then they are
not justified by the argument and still stand in need of valida-
tion. In this respect, religious premisses have no greater logical
force in leading to ethical conclusions than premisses of any
other non-ethical kind. It is not uncommon to find in Christian
apologetic literature arguments purporting to base moral
obligation on the relationship between God as creator and
man as dependent on God. Mr. Nowell Smith in his recent
book on moral philosophy quotes and refutes an argument of
this sort. The argument quoted is from *Christian Ethics* by
the Bishop of Exeter, the Right Rev. Dr. R. C. Mortimer.

> 'God made us and all the world. *Because of that* He has an
> absolute claim on our obedience. We do not exist in our own
> right but only as His creatures who ought therefore to do
> and be what He desires.' This argument requires the premise
> that a creature ought to obey his creator, which is itself a
> moral judgment. So that Christian ethics is not founded
> solely on the doctrine that God created us.[1]

For it is by no means obviously true that the fact, if it is a
fact, that we are created by God and dependent on him,
entails anything at all about our duties. It would no doubt be
imprudent for a creature to ignore the wishes of his creator.
But to say that action is imprudent is not obviously the same
thing as to say that it is wrong.

There is then no reason at all to believe that there is a
connexion of a logical kind between the rules of morality and
certain theological statements such that the former are en-
tailed by the latter. And it would be a sufficient answer to one
who claimed that there was such a connexion to challenge him
to demonstrate it. For such a demonstration, though often
taken for granted, has never been produced. And this is very

[1] P. H. Nowell Smith, *Ethics*, pp. 37–38.

odd. For the usual way to show that a disputed statement is provable is to prove it. What Hume's argument does for us here is to save us wasting time looking for a proof by showing why it could never be found.

But the claim that there is not a *logical* but an *empirical* or *factual* connexion between moral laws and their supposed religious basis is not nearly so easy to refute. It is for that reason more commonly maintained. Let us see what this claim involves. Most of the laws of nature discovered by scientists are statements about the way in which nature usually behaves. There is no logical necessity about them. Given the axioms and definitions of Euclidean geometry, it *is* logically necessary that the square on the hypotenuse of a right triangle is equal to the sum of the squares on the other two sides. Given that there are at least seven million inhabitants of London and that no one has as many as seven million hairs on his head, it *is* logically necessary that there are at least two persons in London with the same number of hairs on their heads.[1] We can know this without doing any counting at all, just as we can know the truth of Pythagoras' theorem without doing any measuring. In other words, these statements are logically necessary, not, of course, taken by themselves but *relative to the premises which are their evidence.* But the case is quite different with the facts and the laws of nature. It is a fact that sodium chloride is a white crystalline substance, that cyanides are poisonous, that penicillin inhibits the growth of bacteria and so on, for countless generalizations about the behaviour of the natural world. But these facts are in no way necessary relative to their evidence. Their evidence is human experience and our past experience can never *guarantee* what our future experience will be, though luckily for us, it is a fairly reliable indication of it. Now is it not possible that the connexion between morality and religion is of this familiar sort? The suggestion is that, human nature being what it is, men will not as a rule accept

[1] A simpler example: if five people each draw a card from an ordinary pack of fifty-two, at least two of them will draw a card of the same suit.

Philosophy of Education

moral principles and act upon them unless such principles are part of the code of their accepted religion. On this view, a good atheist or agnostic would simply be a rather improbable natural phenomenon, just as it would be if we found heather growing on chalky soil or a rose bearing blue flowers.

This suggestion has the merit of being open to the check of experience. It is perhaps strange that it should often be so confidently advanced without any evidence in its favour but at least it is, in principle, provable by observation. The main part of the evidence relevant to it would be a very exhaustive survey of the religious beliefs and the moral professions and practices of a large sample of human beings together with an accurate statistical assessment of the extent to which religion and morality were associated. This would be an immensely complex and difficult task and needless to say it has never been undertaken.[1]

[1] There is a certain amount of factual evidence available on this question, though nothing like enough to justify any sort of dogmatism. The evidence is of two kinds.

(a) Social anthropologists have investigated the moral codes and the religious institutions of a large number of so-called 'primitive' peoples and have found that the relations between morality and religion vary widely from one society to another. (See the evidence summarized in A. Macbeath, *Experiments in Living* (London, 1952).)

(b) There is also a certain amount of sociological evidence though it is not easy to interpret. (Interpretation would need expert statistical treatment.) For example, it has been shown that although Roman Catholics constitute only about 8 per cent of the population of this country, 26 per cent of the women in Holloway Prison and 23 per cent of boys in Borstal institutions are Roman Catholics and that in the Army during the second world war, delinquency was twice as high among Roman Catholics as among non-Catholics. (See *The Tablet*, August 6, 1955, A. G. Rose, *Five Hundred Borstal Boys* (Oxford, 1954), and J. Trenaman, *Out of Step* (London, 1952).) A report on juvenile delinquency to the Bradford Education Committee in 1942 gave the delinquency rate for a representative Roman Catholic school as 15·3 per 1000 while rates for presumably comparable Church of England and non-denominational schools were 7·5 and 6·6 respectively.

It is a truth of sociology, if indeed it is a truth at all, that religion is a precondition of morality. It must therefore be tested by the empirical methods appropriate to such a claim. But in view of the difficulties of measuring the extent to which men conform to their accepted moral codes, it is never likely to be conclusively tested. Such claims are easily made by journalists or zealous churchmen but to collect the only sort of evidence which has a bearing on them is a very formidable project. And even were we to overcome the technical difficulties of collecting the evidence for this thesis and find that there is in fact a significant association between accepting a particular religion and adhering to its moral code, the case would still be far from being established. We should have next to show that religious faith was the cause and moral behaviour the effect. For it might well be that an association between faith and morals were both the result of some third factor such as the temperament of the conformer or his social background.

But suppose that sociologists had collected the evidence for us and evaluated it and that their results were favourable to the hypothesis that morality depended on religious faith of some specific kind. We should still be faced with a further difficulty. Most people who make the claim that religion is the foundation of morals do not mean merely that the acceptance of *any* moral code needs *some* religion as its foundation. Since there are many moral codes and many religions they mean

---

Part of the explanation of these figures may be that Roman Catholics are on the whole poorer than members of other religious groups and are, for that reason, more likely to figure in criminal statistics. Similar figures are however available from Holland where Roman Catholics are not, at present, much poorer than non-Catholics. However these figures are to be interpreted, we can at least say that the present available evidence does not *support* the suggestion that membership of the largest of the Christian Churches is conducive to a higher standard of conduct than that of unbelievers. We can say this while recognizing that wickedness is not quite the same as criminality.

I am indebted for these figures to Mrs. Margaret Knight of the Department of Psychology in the University of Aberdeen.

rather that *true* morality needs *true* religion to guarantee it in this way. Naturally enough, this means that the morality which they recognize requires the religion which they profess. And this very specific claim raises all the philosophical difficulties about the proof of ethical and metaphysical statements that we have already discussed. For it would involve us in attempting to prove that a specific moral code is *the* right one for man and that a particular form of religion was true and that all others were false. And this certainly has never been done and, for the reasons we have already considered, is never likely to be. Thus if we ask ourselves what sort of evidence would be necessary to establish the so far unproved assertion that morality needs a foundation in religion, we see that it requires (*a*) a large scale piece of sociological research of a very difficult and complex kind; (*b*) an agreed settlement of the fundamental philosophical problems of morality and natural religion. It is one thing to assert as a 'self-evident truth' that morality needs a religious background and quite another to collect even a little evidence in its favour.

Fortunately, we need not undertake the task of amassing and evaluating factual evidence on this question for there are philosophical arguments to suggest that there is no important connexion between morality and religion. There is, of course, no reason to deny the well-established fact that a sincere believer will tend to be a moral man in the sense that he will try to conform to the moral rules of the religion that he professes. This is, indeed, almost a tautology, since it is part of the definition of a sincere believer that he does this. But the sceptic can confront the believer with the following dilemma: 'Either you believe that moral good and evil are good and evil *because God says they are*, or you believe that they are independent of God's will. And both of these alternatives will be found unacceptable to you.' Let us look more closely at this challenge.

When a religious man says that he tries to be kind or chaste or generous because it is God's will that he should act in this way, he does not usually mean that God has laid down arbit-

132

rarily that men should behave so. He usually means rather that
God demands this sort of conduct because it is good and not
that it is good because God demands it. When Hamlet wished:

> 'that the Everlasting had not fixed
> His canon 'gainst self-slaughter'

he seemed to imply that suicide was wrong because God had
issued an edict against it. But this has not usually been held to
be the Christian view of morals. The theory of natural law
which has played such an important part in Christian philosophy would have been quite superfluous had the theologians
commonly held that morality was merely a set of divine edicts.[1]
The leading Christian thinkers, Protestant and Roman Catholic
alike, have all held that good and bad conduct were good and
bad for quite other reasons than God's approval and disapproval, though naturally they have believed that God did in
fact approve of good conduct and disapprove of bad. Indeed,
they have held that he expresses and reinforces his approvals
and disapprovals with substantial rewards and punishments.

The matter of God's approval or disapproval is then quite
irrelevant to the rightness or wrongness of a certain type of
conduct. As we have seen, it is a very difficult philosophical
question to decide why right actions are right and wrong
actions wrong. But however we settle this issue, provided we
do not say that right acts are right *because God says so*, there
can be only one morally good reason for doing a good action,
namely, that it is good, just as there is only one morally good
reason for refraining from a bad one. If it can be shown that
God approves of the good action, that is an interesting fact
about it; but it is not an additional reason for doing it. For we
have in the goodness of the action all the reason we need.
Similarly we do not need the assurance of God's disapproval
to give us a moral reason for refraining from a bad action. For
its badness is itself an adequate reason, and the only adequate
reason, for refraining. For if the action was not bad, though

[1] Only a few of them have held this. The best known of these
was the eighteenth-century English divine, Paley.

divine disapproval might provide an excellent *prudential* motive for resisting temptation, it could never provide a *moral* reason.

Thus the believer and the unbeliever are on equal terms in the matter of moral conduct. Each has the same good and sufficient reason for acting rightly, namely, that the action is right. The believer may of course have additional *incentives* for acting rightly. He may love God and wish for that reason to do what God wills. Or less creditably, he may fear God's punishments or be anxious to qualify for his rewards. But these motives neither make acts right or wrong if they are not so already, nor do they add to the moral worth of good acts nor increase the iniquity of bad ones. For this to be the case, it would have to be true that the mere act of conforming with the divine will, irrespective of what that will prescribes, is itself a morally good act. And this is neither self-evidently true nor could it ever be proved to be true.[1] Thus God's wishes in the matter of moral conduct, even if they could be shown to exist, must be morally irrelevant.

Nevertheless, the fact that religion provides incentives (though not good reasons) for acting morally has often been used to support a modified claim about the necessity of religion to morality. It is said that morality needs sanctions if it is to be taken seriously by most of mankind and such sanctions can only be provided, when they are not embodied in the laws and conventions of society, by the threats and promises of divine justice. If men come to disbelieve in the religious backing for moral conduct, they will cease to act morally. For though no doubt they *ought* to act virtuously without any external incentive, most men will not do so. But this claim is of course just the old sociological thesis that we have already considered. And we have seen the sort of evidence that would be needed to make it plausible. Moreover, this modified claim raises a moral issue. Suppose that we could prove that adherence to a certain religion does tend to encourage good behaviour, would it then follow that the religion should be given a privileged position

[1] See page 128 above.

in the social structure, taught to children and maintained as the orthodox creed? Is it not rather the case that religious truths, if such exist, must be maintained and propagated on the ground that they are *true* and not merely that they are *useful*? And their truth can certainly not be proved merely by demonstrating that they are what Lord Chesterfield called 'the collateral security for virtue'. Some authoritarian thinkers, of whom Plato is the most notable, have recommended rulers to tell useful lies to their subjects as a device of government. But to most men such devices seem not only wrong but despicable. If a religion is true *and can be shown to be so* then it should be taught, whether or not its effects are fortunate. And if it cannot be shown to be true then it ought not to be propagated officially, even though its social consequences are excellent.

It is worth mentioning a practical disadvantage that has sometimes been urged against the close association of morals and religion that we have been considering. The point has no bearing on the *truth* of the thesis that morality and religion are essentially connected, but it is an interesting one and is usually overlooked by those who wish to maintain that such a connexion exists. If morality is believed to need religion for its foundation and to be insecure without it, the moral standards of a community will suffer needlessly if, for any reason, the religion comes to be widely disbelieved. Now this may very easily happen to a religion, for good reasons or for bad. For example, Christianity as a system of theology has lost much of its hold on the minds of educated men in western Europe during the past two hundred years. And this change of attitude can be shown to be closely connected with the rise of natural science since the sixteenth century.[1] This is not to say that scientific discoveries have any tendency to *disprove* Christian doctrines except when such doctrines have been incautiously stated as if they were scientific theories. But the rise of science has created an intellectual atmosphere that has proved to be

[1] For an excellent discussion of this, see Professor W. T. Stace's book *Religion and the Modern Mind*, in particular, Chapters 1–7.

unfavourable to the Christian way of looking at the world. This has resulted in the doctrines losing some of their credibility. And to the extent that the doctrines are, quite wrongly, believed to be necessary as the guarantees of moral rules, no doubt the moral rules have also come to lose some of their authority. It is, as I have suggested above, quite impossible to assess the extent of this loss or even to be sure that it has occurred. But if it has, it may very well be attributed to the false belief that there is an essential link between religion and morality. If then morality is undeservedly involved in the discredit of theology, this may be attributed as much to the bad logic of believers as to any other cause.

V

This sort of criticism of the function of religion is sometimes objected to nòt on the ground that it is logically unjustified but rather because an impersonal and critical attitude is inappropriate to a discussion of these matters. Religion and morality do, after all, concern the everyday conduct of our lives. And since everyone, including the most sceptical of philosophers, has to live, the philosophers cannot take up this attitude to all rules of living. Do they claim to live by no rules at all or to exempt their own rules from critical scrutiny? Different philosophers would no doubt answer this question in different ways. (I have given one answer to it at the end of Section III above.) It is however worth reminding ourselves that once we appeal to philosophy to give some rational colouring to our religious beliefs, we must be very careful in using this sort of objection. Anyone who invites the verdict of reason must be prepared, if his invitation is made in good faith, to accept the verdict whichever way it goes. He may indeed re-examine such a verdict in the light of reason but he may reject it only if he can identify some logical error in the argument that leads to it. It is open to any believer to exempt his beliefs from that verdict by claiming that they do not rest on ordinary communicable evidence and are therefore beyond the reach of reason. There is nowadays an increasing number of believers who are prepared to take this attitude. But they do so only by renouncing reason altogether in the religious sphere; and such a renunciation in so important a matter brings its own dangers.

I have been concerned here only with the claim that education has a necessary basis in ethics and religion and that it is the task of philosophy to justify this claim by making clear the character of the connexion. I believe that it is true that morality has this essential link with education but that it is false that religion is relevant at all. And I have tried to show how this belief might be justified by a very cursory philosophical criticism of the crucial questions: (i) 'What is the purpose of man?' (ii) 'What is the relation between religion and morals?' To the first question, the answer seems to be: 'Man has no purpose in living except those that he himself puts into his life. Such purposes may be trivial and selfish but often they are not. They need not be, nor indeed *ought* they to be so.' To the second question, I should answer: 'It can be shown that there is no necessary or logical connexion between religion and morals and it has not been shown that there is any empirical connexion. In any case, to make the concept of moral obligation dependent on God's will is to remove the essential feature of the concept. We ought to do right and to refrain from doing wrong whether or not there is a God and whether or not he has any moral preferences at all. If these preferences exist, they are morally irrelevant. If they are believed to exist, they may act as non-moral incentives for action but that is the most that can be said.'

Such a position has the logical virtue of making few positive presuppositions. It is thus in a much stronger position than the religious claim I have rejected; for this can very easily be shown to be logically vulnerable and, in any ordinary sense of the word 'evidence', to have no positive evidence in its favour. Moreover, the practical results of separating morals from religion in this way have not been shown to be worse than the results of maintaining the connexion. If a religious man takes morality seriously, he will live well but so will an unbeliever who does the same. And the unbeliever will be in no danger of jettisoning his moral rules if his theology comes to seem doubtful. For he has no theology. I am not concerned here with the claim that a non-religious morality is *psychologically* impossible for the average man and it is therefore essential to the stability of society that some sort of religion, irrespective of its truth, should be publicly professed as a measure of social hygiene. So far as they are factual, these are statements that fall within the province of psychology and sociology. Even if they were true (and so far there has not been any serious attempt to collect evidence for them) the value statement implicit in them is morally objectionable. And for that reason it is not one that most religious persons would be willing to maintain.

VI

I shall conclude by summarizing those points of contact between education and philosophy that comprise what might properly be called 'the philosophy of education'. There is first the question of the way in which judgments of value, and in particular of moral value, may be criticized and clarified. This was very sketchily treated in Chapter 3. It will have been obvious however that a serious treatment of this question involves a serious study of moral philosophy as a whole. There is secondly what might be called the logic of explanation. This is an examination of the nature of theories and, in particular of educational theories, so that we may be more fully aware, in our study of such theories, of what they are attempting to do. Chapters 4 and 5 give a very elementary outline of this subject. Thirdly, there is a set of basic questions in the philosophy of religion that have been discussed at a very elementary level in the present chapter. Lastly, there is the very difficult and controversial question of the nature of philosophical enquiry of which a rather superficial and admittedly partial account was given in Chapter 2. For until we get our minds clear on the nature of philosophy, we shall not be clear about questions in the philosophy of education. In short, there is no such 'subject' as the philosophy of education any more than there is such a 'subject' as the philosophy of science. But to say this is not to discredit these enquiries. It merely points to the fact that these studies are fragments of a larger whole. There are genuine and very important philosophical problems that are the concern of students of education just as there are problems in philosophy which specially interest students of the sciences. And it is useful that these problems should be brought together and discussed under one title so that students should be aware that such problems exist and that they are philosophical. They are bound to be discussed in any case and it is therefore important that their nature should be appreciated. For no philosophizing is more inept than that which is done unconsciously.

But it must be remembered that all the problems of philosophy are linked together in such a way that the most remote and abstruse problem in the theory of knowledge may be relevant to the question of the existence of God or to the problems of morals and politics. This means that no part of philosophy can be separated from the rest except merely for convenience. In introducing philosophy to students of education, we have to make a different selection of problems from the one which would interest students of science or of history. But wherever we begin, we shall be led in the end to the same places. Philosophy is much more of a unity than its controversies would suggest. If we realize this, we shall also realize the futility of criticisms of contemporary philosophy by the intellectual journalists of the day. They complain that philosophers no longer deal with 'the great problems' of God and human destiny but concern themselves instead with pointless arguments over the meanings of words or over such curious queries as whether tables really exist or how we know that other people think and feel as we do. Anyone who has even an elementary acquaintance with philosophical thinking knows very well that the outcome of such seemingly trivial enquiries has a determining influence on our philosophizing about God and human destiny. Criticism of philosophers for their academic detachment and their interest in the minutiae of the theory of knowledge or the philosophy of language is just as ill-informed as criticism of mathematicians for spending their time in the specialities of pure mathematics. Just as there can be no advances in physics or engineering without previous work in pure mathematics, so there can be no effective thinking about morals or politics or natural religion unless more basic issues in philosophy have first been settled. And this is, of course, not a discovery of recent philosophers. The metaphysicians of Greek and medieval times were well aware of it.

Thus the problems of the philosophy of education, if pressed far enough, become the traditional problems of philosophy. Those questions that have been treated in the preceding pages are merely the most obvious points of entry to the field of philosophy for someone with interests in educational theory. There are, of course, equally important questions that have not been discussed. For example, the controversies about free will and responsibility, about the nature of the mind and its relation to the body, about conceptual thinking and about the self are also important both in their own right and in relation to education. But I shall do no more than mention them here.[1] They are perhaps too complex and difficult to be suitable for a very elementary book of this kind. There are also problems of social philosophy concerning the relation between the individual and society which have a very direct bearing on the structure of an educational system and on the content of what is taught.[2] It thus becomes largely a matter of convenience to decide how much of the whole field of philosophy we are prepared to include in what we wish to call 'the philosophy of education'. What has been discussed in the preceding pages is intended only to serve as an introduction to a very much wider field.

[1] For elementary treatments of these questions, see Bibliographical Note to Chapter 2.

[2] See the references in the Bibliographical Note to Chapter 3.

BIBLIOGRAPHICAL NOTES

(*N.B.* The numbers in brackets refer to the Bibliography on pages 143–44)

Chapter 1. Most books on the philosophy of education do not distinguish sufficiently between strictly philosophical questions and those disputes about either fact or value that may arise in questions of educational theory and practice. They have therefore to be read with care unless they are to give a false and confused idea of philosophy. Standard books on the philosophy of education are Dewey (8), Lodge (22) and Brubacher (3). Butler (5) gives an account of the relations between certain philosophical viewpoints and theories of education. The only attempt by a philosopher to clarify educational theory by means of philosophy is Hardie (15). This is an excellent book written with a clarity quite exceptional in educational writings. It is unfortunately out of print.

Chapter 2. The notion that philosophy is a process of analysis is a modern one but examples of its practice can be found in all the classical philosophers from Plato onwards. However, it is difficult for the student to disentangle such examples from the less valuable parts of classical writings. The best introduction to modern philosophical thinking is probably still Russell (27). Whiteley (36) and Woozley (38) give good beginners' accounts of the main problems of philosophy from a more consciously analytical standpoint. Hospers (16) is the only easy and systematic introduction to philosophical analysis and this can be followed by Pap (25). This is a more difficult book and contains some original discussions of traditional problems. Ayer (1) is a classic among recent philosophical writings and gives a brilliant exposition of an extreme anti-metaphysical point of view. For specimens of the work of the linguistic school of analysis, see Flew (11) and (12). Appreciation of much recent philosophy needs an elementary knowledge of modern logic such as is given in Basson and O'Connor (2) or Langer (21). The most readable account of the history of philosophy is Russell (28) but its reliability is sometimes sacrificed to entertainment. The best short account of the rise of modern science is Butterfield (6).

Chapter 3. The simplest introduction to ethics is Ewing (9). This should be followed by one or two of the standard works of moral philosophy, say, Butler (4), Hume (18), Mill (23) and Moore (24). The student should then be ready for some of the recent approaches to ethics. These begin with Chapter 4 of Ayer (1) and Stevenson (33). Toulmin (34) is a valuable examination of the nature of ethical reasoning. Hare (14) and Nowell Smith (30) develop the linguistic approach to morals first treated by Stevenson. Neither of these are easy but they are both important and original books which will have an influence on the development of ethics. Hospers and Sellars (17) is a collection of recent papers on moral philosophy and gives a good idea of current trends. Schlick (29) is a simple positivist approach to ethics which has been unduly neglected. A very readable account of the problems of social and political thinking is given by Weldon (35), though this is more helpful as a criticism of wrong approaches to political theory than as a constructive essay.

Chapter 4. Discussion of theories and explanations will be found in standard text-books on logic and scientific method. The most useful of these are Cohen and Nagel (7), Stebbing (32) and Wisdom (37). Chapter 3 of Hospers (16) has a good discussion of explanation and hypothesis. Hutten (19) has an excellent account of the role played by models in science.

Chapter 5. Kaufmann (20) deals with the problems of theory and explanation in the social sciences. Some very valuable original treatment of these problems will be found in Popper (26). There has been little critical discussion of theory-making in education apart from Hardie (15) and Feigl (10).

Chapter 6. Stace (31) is a clear and stimulating discussion of some problems in the philosophy of religion. This is a more sympathetic account than will be found in most contemporary philosophers. It gives a useful sketch of the historical background to changes in religious attitude over the past three hundred years. Recent philosophical discussion of the problems of the philosophy of religion can be found in Flew and MacIntyre (13).

BIBLIOGRAPHY

1   Ayer, A. J. *Language, Truth and Logic* (Second Edition). London, 1946.
2   Basson, A. H., and O'Connor, D. J. *Introduction to Symbolic Logic* (Second Edition). London, 1957.
3   Brubacher, J. S. *Modern Philosophies of Education*. New York, 1950.
4   Butler, J. *Fifteen Sermons*. London, 1914.
5   Butler, J. D. *Four Philosophies and their Practice in Education and Religion*. Princeton, 1951.
6   Butterfield, H. *The Origins of Modern Science, 1300 to 1800*. London, 1949.
7   Cohen, M. R., and Nagel, E. *Introduction to Logic and Scientific Method*. London, 1951.
8   Dewey, J. *Democracy and Education: An Introduction to Philosophy of Education*. New York, 1916.
9   Ewing, A. C. *Ethics*. London, 1953.
10 Feigl, H. 'Aims of Education for our Age' in *Modern Philosophies and Education*. Chicago, 1955.
11 Flew, A. G. N. *Essays on Logic and Language* (First Series). Oxford, 1951.
12 Flew, A. G. N. *Essays on Logic and Language* (Second Series). Oxford, 1953.
13 Flew, A. G. N., and MacIntyre, A. C. *New Essays in Philosophical Theology*. London, 1955.
14 Hare, R. M. *The Language of Morals*. Oxford, 1952.
15 Hardie, C. D. *Truth and Fallacy in Educational Theory*. Cambridge, 1942.
16 Hospers, J. *Introduction to Philosophical Analysis*. London, 1956.
17 Hospers, J., and Sellars, W. S. *Readings in Ethical Theory*. New York, 1953.

Bibliography

18 Hume, D. *Selections* (edited by C. W. Hendel). New York, 1927.

19 Hutten, E. H. *The Language of Modern Physics*. London, 1955.

20 Kaufmann, F. *The Methodology of the Social Sciences*. London, 1944.

21 Langer, S. K. *An Introduction to Symbolic Logic*. London, 1937.

22 Lodge, R. C. *Philosophy of Education*. New York, 1947.

23 Mill, J. S. *Utilitarianism* (Everyman's Library). London, 1931.

24 Moore, G. E. *Ethics*. London, 1912.

25 Pap, A. *Elements of Analytic Philosophy*. New York, 1949.

26 Popper, K. R. *The Open Society and its Enemies* (Two volumes). London, 1945.

27 Russell, B. A. W. *The Problems of Philosophy*. London, 1912.

28 Russell, B. A. W. *The History of Western Philosophy*. London, 1946.

29 Schlick, M. *The Problems of Ethics*. New York, 1949.

30 Smith, P. H. Nowell. *Ethics*. London, 1953.

31 Stace, W. T. *Religion and the Modern Mind*. London, 1953.

32 Stebbing, L. S. *A Modern Introduction to Logic*. London, 1953.

33 Stevenson, C. L. *Ethics and Language*. New Haven, 1944.

34 Toulmin, S. E. *The Place of Reason in Ethics*. Cambridge, 1950.

35 Weldon, T. D. *The Vocabulary of Politics*. London, 1933.

36 Whiteley, C. H. *An Introduction to Metaphysics*. London, 1950.

37 Wisdom, J. O. *Foundations of Inference in Natural Science*. London, 1952.

38 Woozley, A. D. *Theory of Knowledge: An Introduction*. London, 1949.

INDEX

Index